Ten Steps for Genuine Leadership in Schools

This book provides busy educators with insight on genuine processes and decision-making that maximizes student learning and overall academic success. Full of examples, templates, reflective prompts, and suggestions on how to plan for and drive daily practice, *Ten Steps for Genuine Leadership in Schools* explores the importance of a genuine learning environment, genuine instructional practices, genuine innovative processes, a genuine vision and mission of your school, and genuine relationships between staff, students, parents, and community. Covering specific strategies that can be implemented immediately, this book is a straightforward and honest approach in doing what really matters in the principal's chair to elicit positive student outcomes.

David M. Fultz is an administrator in the West Clermont School District in Ohio and an Educational Consultant for Ohio State University, USA.

D1525424

Ten Steps for Genuine Leadership in Schools

David M. Fultz

Routledge
Taylor & Francis Group

NEW YORK AND LONDON

First published 2017
by Routledge
711 Third Avenue, New York, NY 10017

and by Routledge
2 Park Square, Milton Park, Abingdon, Oxon, OX14 4RN

Routledge is an imprint of the Taylor & Francis Group, an informa business

© 2017 Taylor & Francis

Library of Congress Cataloging in Publication Data
A catalog record for this book has been requested

ISBN: 978-1-138-22358-5 (hbk)
ISBN: 978-1-138-22359-2 (pbk)
ISBN: 978-1-315-40438-7 (ebk)

Typeset in Optima
by Apex CoVantage, LLC

I would like to thank my parents, Richard and Sandra Fultz, for instilling in me a work ethic of enduring quality and diligence while working toward any endeavor my heart desires. They sacrificed so that I could achieve my dreams.

I would like to thank Jeanne Hornberger for being that critical friend, pushing me to improve upon my professional self and challenging me to be a better leader, educator, and writer.

I would like to thank my children, Abigail, Magdalena, Evelyn, and Emma for being my cheerleaders, and for keeping me grounded by their constant reminder that every student I work with is someone's son or daughter. I also want to give a special thanks to Abigail and Magdalena for their artistic influence in this book.

Finally, I would like to say thank you to my wife, Agnes Fultz. Your continual love and support helped me through this process.

Contents

Preface

Genuine leadership is a straightforward and honest approach
in doing what really matters to elicit positive student outcomes.

Education is the largest running social program in the United States, as it
is based on compulsory attendance in all states, usually from the ages of 5
to 18. Every child regardless of race, ethnicity, gender, class, special need,
nationality, and socio-economic status is mandated to attend some form
of structured educational process. One of my favorite quotes supporting
the concept behind compulsory education was from British politician (and
early education supporter for all children) Baron Henry Peter Brougham. In
the 1700s he was quoted (Goodreads, 2015) as saying, "Education makes
people easy to lead but difficult to drive; easy to govern but impossible
to enslave." In other words, educated individuals will not follow blindly
down a path towards chaos and destruction, but will recognize the difference between good and evil, AND will choose good.

John Kennedy also focused on the need for a strong educational system
in order to support a robust and fruitful nation. He said (Quotationspage,
2015), "Let us think of education as the means of developing our greatest
abilities, because in each of us there is a private hope and dream which,
fulfilled, can be translated into benefit for everyone and greater strength
for our nation." We educate to strengthen the individual. We educate to
strengthen the nation. Through the process of education, we ensure the
survival and success of our future.

We must understand that education is not equal or equitable, but
"standard." What we implement and assess in schools are based on standards set forth by our individual state departments of education, as well as

our local educational agencies. Standards, and benchmarks to assess those standards, are paramount in demonstrating student achievement and overall school success. As an educational leader, you have a hand in cultivating an environment where students must demonstrate success and successfully progress through their educational career towards a profession that will allow them to be productive citizens of this nation.

What the Book Is About

Genuine leadership in action is a straightforward and honest approach in doing what really matters in the principal's chair to elicit positive student outcomes. This book contains information on how you, as your school's "sentinel of education," can tap into resources (including physical, financial, and human capital) and cultivate an environment where students are achieving at a level and degree far beyond a "standard" education. This book provides insight on genuine processes and decision-making on how to network information, stakeholders, and resources in a way that maximizes student learning and overall academic success.

Who the Book Is For

This book is a blueprint for you to become the school leader that you have always wanted to be but couldn't quite figure out how to get there. As you will find throughout this book, the answers to complicated or philosophical questions often start with the simplest of ideas. You are the driving force for success. You are what makes the difference at the school. You are the curator of the culture and the captain of the ship. Between these chapters are what you need to know and do in order to become a genuine leader.

How This Book Is Organized

As the title illustrates, this book is organized around 10 steps in genuine leadership in schools. These steps aren't necessarily in chronological order but rather grouped in constructs identified as 4 principles, 3 processes, 2 goals, and 1 rule. Each chapter, delineating each step, include examples, reflections, and templates that drive the reader to go beyond the consumption of knowledge, by truly putting genuine leadership into their daily practice. Engaging in these actions will enhance the impact of the contents of this book and assist you in developing your heightened sense of awareness of your leadership.

Special Features

Throughout this book, you will find special features that allow you to truly reflect on what you just read and plan for action. Each chapter ends with a heading titled "Chapter Takeaways." These sections include the main tidbit of knowledge essential for that chapter. It also lists the templates used in each chapter to expound upon the presented topics. Further, it includes takeaway tasks that will allow you to begin lifting the knowledge from the pages and putting that knowledge into your specific practice. Finally, there is a moment of reflection. This section allows you to take that deep breath, look inward upon your thoughts and practices, and truly reflect on where you want to develop as a genuine leader.

References

Goodreads. (2015). Retrieved 2015 from http://www.goodreads.com/quotes/18783-education-makes-a-people-easy-to-lead-but-difficult-to

Quotationspage. (2015). Retrieved October 23, 2015 from http://www.quotationspage.com/quote/8280.html

eResources

Keep an eye out for the eResources icon throughout this book, which indicates a resource is available online. Resources mentioned in this book can be downloaded, printed, used to copy/paste text, and/or manipulated to suit your individualized use. You can access these downloads by visiting the book product page on our website:

www.routledge.com/products/9781138223592

Then click on the tab that reads "eResources" and then select the file(s) you need. The file(s) will download directly to your computer.

Introduction

What Is Genuine Leadership?

Genuine leadership is not the absence of instructional leadership, but rather its complement.

School Leaders

Before we get into what it means to be a genuine leader, we must first recognize the impact that school leaders have on teachers and students. The leader of the school plays a significant role in creating an environment where students can achieve. Leithwood, Seashore Louis, Anderson, and Walstrom (2004) identify leadership as the pivotal point in improving student learning.

> Leadership is widely regarded as a key factor in accounting for difference in the success with which schools foster the learning of their students. Indeed, the contribution of effective leadership is largest when it is needed most: there are virtually no documented instances of troubled schools being turned around in the absence of intervention by talented leaders. While other factors within the school also contribute to such turnarounds, leadership is the catalyst.
>
> (p. 17)

Likewise, Lezotte (1994) identifies the principal as the dominant power that influences student academic success. He states:

> When one asks who decides how resources such as time and limited money get allocated, the answer in most schools is, "the

principal". If one asks who decides what and who gets praised and sanctioned, the answer in most schools is, "the principal". When someone asks who places students in different settings, sets priorities for the future, creates the climate and expectations for the school, and recruits and socializes new teachers, again the answer is, "the principal". Taken together, these elements constitute a force powerful enough to alter what has been the normal flow of that school.

(p. 22)

Prior and current research into the effectiveness of the school leader has proven fruitful. Much of it demonstrates that the school leader has a positive impact on student success. A significant part of this impact is more directly related to their focus on curriculum and instructional practices (Blase & Blase, 2002; Leithwood & Riehl, 2003; Marzano, Waters, & McNulty, 2005). Another factor is that the school leader has a large impact on setting the direction of the school, developing people, redesigning the culture and structure of the organization, being visible and a good communicator and collaborator (Andrews & Soder, 1987; Cotton, 2003; Leithwood et al., 2004)

There is a plethora of philosophies and data that clearly indicate that the principal has a strong impact (directly and indirectly) on student learning and a strong overall impact (directly) on the climate of the school building. It has been established that their influence is widespread and powerful, with the instructional focus being essential to their success. Although past research has parceled out the term "instructional leader" to describe a "style" or "type" of leader, this allowed other types or styles to also compete for the school leader's attention. In this current era of educational accountability, the focus of instruction has evolved. The mindful focus on instruction can no longer be viewed as a "type" or "style" of leadership, but rather an essential piece of all leaders' daily practice of running a school. Instruction must be cognizant in every thought the school leader has, and embedded in every decision the leader makes that affects the school.

Given the inherent and intentional focus on instruction by the school leader, we must consider what other characteristics need to be in place to complement instruction in order to maximize student success. With that instructional focus being the core, the most significant question then becomes, "What type of leader should one be in order to elicit the most positive influence on staff, students, and the school environment as a whole?" I propose it is that of a *genuine* leader.

Genuine Leadership

Merriam-Webster online dictionary defines **genuine** as, "Sincere and honest: Actual, real and true: Not false or fake" (2016). Genuine is often identified as a character trait in an individual that presents themselves in a clear, straightforward manner. It is someone who emanates honesty, integrity, and true care and concern for others' feelings, ideas, and input. Educational leaders who exude genuineness often find teachers drawn to their ideas, passion, and vision for education. Teachers find themselves compelled to follow them and facilitate the attainment of their greater goals and objectives.

James Comer (1995) once said, "No significant learning occurs without a significant relationship." A genuine leader understands that relations are at the fundamental level of all learning and sustained success. These relationships are not bound by status, rank, or experience but rather by mutual respect, expertise, and heartfelt support for one another. Therefore, the concept of "Genuine Leadership" is the clear and straightforward stewardship of education through the tight and loosely coupled relationships between concepts, content, and people that support student success.

Genuine leadership is also not about following any one theory per se, but rather having the flexibility to put together a variety of principles, processes, goals, and necessary actions that create and facilitate positive, sustained student outcomes. These pieces are not thrown together haphazardly but exist within a network built upon the connected relationships between the principal, staff, students, parents, and local community. This environment fluctuates to meld to any given situation.

When administrators engage in a genuine approach to leadership, they cultivate a school climate in which the teachers are impacted by the influence of the collective capacity of the school community, which in turn evokes positive outcomes on student academic success (Seashore Louis, Leithwood, Wahlstrom, & Anderson, 2010). An administrator who utilizes genuine leadership engages in the learning environment, monitors teacher practices, maintains the flow of support and resources to where they are needed, develops innovative processes for learning, and stewards the vision and mission of the school. Genuine leadership is not the absence of instructional leadership, but rather its complement. In a genuine leadership approach, the school leader elicits the greatest impact on student academic success through building school capacity, fostering teacher knowledge development, and supporting teacher-led collaborative learning teams. In this manner, the school leader facilitates the networking of ideas, practices, processes, and supports so that students reap the benefits of efficient and effective exchanges of teaching information, techniques, and best practices.

As the title suggests, there are 10 steps for genuine leadership:

Step 1: Keep Your Focus on the Child
Step 2: Share Your Vision, NOT Your Brain
Step 3: Understand That Absolute Power Corrupts Absolutely
Step 4: Education Is a "Contact" Sport
Step 5: Know What You Have / Know What Need
Step 6: Building Network Capacity
Step 7: Know Your Role
Step 8: Cultivate Student Success
Step 9: Cultivate Teacher Satisfaction
Step 10: Treat Others Like You Want to Be Treated

The corresponding chapters go into each step in greater detail.

Moment of Reflection . . .

What do I believe is genuine about me personally that directly influences my professionalism? How does this influence my leadership abilities and the school environment?

_____

_____

_____

_____

Genuine leadership is not the *absence* of instructional leadership, but rather its complement.

References

Andrews, R., & Soder, R. (1987). Principal instructional leadership and school achievement. *Educational Leadership, 44*(6), 9–11.

Blase, J., & Blase, J. (2002). Teachers' perceptions of principals' instructional leadership and implications. *Leadership and Policy in Schools, 1*(3), 256–264.

Comer, J. (1995). *Lecture given at Education Service Center, Region IV.* Houston, TX.

Cotton, K. (2003). *Principals and student achievement: What the research says.* Alexandria, VA: Association for Supervision and Curriculum Development.

Leithwood, K., & Riehl, C. (2003). *What do we already know about successful school leadership?* Paper presented at the annual meeting of the American Educational Research Association.

Leithwood, K., Seashore Louis, K., Anderson, S., & Walstrom, K. (2004). *How leadership influences student learning.* Minneapolis: Center for Applied Research and Educational Improvement, University of Minnesota.

Lezotte, L. (1994). The nexus of instructional leadership. *School Administrator, 51*(6), 20–23.

Marzano, R., Waters, T., & McNulty, B. (2005). *School leadership that works: From research to results.* Alexandria, VA: Association for Supervision and Curriculum Development.

Merriam-Webster. (2016). *Genuine.* Retrieved January 18, 2016 from http://www.merriam-webster.com/dictionary/genuine

Seashore Louis, K., Leithwood, K., Wahlstrom, K., & Anderson, S. (2010). *Investigating the links to improved student learning.* Retrieved June 3, 2010 from http://www.wallacefoundation.org/KnowledgeCenter/Knowledge Topics/CurrentAreasofFocus/EducationLeadership/Pages/learning-from-leadership-investigating-the-links-to-improved-student-learning.aspx

2 | **Know Your Staff**

Get to know your staff on a more genuine level.

Close your eyes and allow your mind to focus on that most recent hire right out of college. Picture that teacher's attributes, skill level, enthusiasm, and general approach to the first day of school. Now, picture your most seasoned teacher and their attributes, skill level, enthusiasm, and general approach to the first day of school. How far apart are these two teachers in terms of knowledge, skills, and dispositions with instructing children, teamwork building, and ability to network with outside organizations? Now, think about the entire range of teachers in your building. Understanding where your teachers are, and what they can do, is important in cultivating genuine leadership.

Teacher personalities and perceptions guide their approach to teaching, as well as the implementation of teaching practices. There are instruments available (many for a cost) that help teachers understand their personalities and how they approach their professional duties. A popular one is the Myers-Briggs Type Indicator (MBTI). The Myers & Briggs Foundation (Myers-Briggs Foundation, 2015) offers the MBTI assessment, which divides individuals into 16 unique types. Leadership styles can also be identified using assessments such as DiSC (Personality Profile Solutions, 2015). DiSC divides styles up into four categories: Dominance, influence, Steadiness, and Conscientiousness. The purpose of this is to improve teamwork, collaboration, and ultimately productivity by identifying behavioral differences, which allows for appropriate personnel development. Like with MBTI, DiSC comes at a cost for which many school districts are not willing to invest. To get a general feel for your staff, without breaking your budget, you as the school leader may find it valuable to look at more open-source researched outcomes. One of these resources can be looking at teachers from a "generational" point of view (Hammill, 2005; Karp, Fuller, & Sirias, 2002; Lancaster & Stillman, 2002; Zemke, Raines, & Filipczak, 2000).

Most teachers in classrooms today were born into three different generations. Although they are not bound to think, feel, and behave in any specific way, it is advantageous for you as a school leader to understand the thoughts, feelings, and ideas that make up the culture of specific generations. The three generations to which I am referring are the Baby Boomers, Generation X, and the Millennials (Hammill, 2005; Karp et al., 2002; Lancaster & Stillman, 2002; Zemke et al., 2000).

Remember that the characteristics of each generation of individuals will be generalizations. I am not claiming that everyone in a specific generation will behave in a certain way. These are meant to be guidelines for you to get some idea of your teachers' thought processes and actions. It is similar to observing a kindergarten class. We could refer to overarching similarities like their ages, heights, and ability to stand in a line when directed. However, when you drill down, some kindergarteners look like first graders, some look like preschoolers, and others act like they should be in kindergarten. Apply this similar logic to the generational identifiers that I am about to discuss.

There are many books, journal articles, and website posts that cover all facets of generational characteristics. This chapter is geared more toward understanding those characteristics so that you as an educational leader can make more informed decisions when working with teachers of different generations. We will briefly be covering the generations. If you want to learn more about each one, please consult the plethora of available media.

Baby Boomers

Baby Boomers are your most experienced teachers. They typically own the culture of the school and are ingrained into the work setting. Before you can influence them and build upon their ability to network with the other generations of teachers, you must first know who they are.

Who Are They?

Baby Boomers were born right after the Great Depression occurred in America. They were raised by parents to value employment, and success was defined by hard work and dedication to their employer. This generation tends to spend their entire work life with one company. They are generally optimistic and involved in their community to make a positive difference. Family is important; however, the nuclear family concept began disintegrating as divorce started to occur more frequently.

Baby Boomers are workaholics who find fulfillment and purpose in their actions. If their job does not provide these, they are more apt to seek fulfillment in hobbies and support causes, rather than change jobs. Work is based on a hierarchical structure and they place value in rank. Face-time with the boss is necessary to get a promotion. Success is achieved using a clever, resourceful, and "strive to win" mentality. A strong work ethic is important and they find satisfaction in being a positive contributor to the success of the organization.

Baby Boomers are individuals who define success by hard work. They believe that dedication to your job and significant sacrifice are perquisites to being successful. Everyone has to pay their dues and there are no meaningful shortcuts to the top. They struggled through all of the pitfalls and setbacks until they found a way to be successful, and are not readily excited about sharing or disclosing to more inexperienced individuals how to avoid such pitfalls. They view stumbling and temporary failure as learning opportunities that everyone must experience (Hammill, 2005; Karp et al., 2002; Lancaster & Stillman, 2002; Zemke et al., 2000).

Leading Them

In order to be successful in your interaction with Baby Boomers, as well as cultivate an educational environment conducive for students to grow, you need to understand how to communicate with them, recognize their contributions, and provide leadership they respect. You must also know how to get them involved and committed to the mission and vision of the school. Baby Boomers want acknowledgement for their knowledge and experience. You as a leader must recognize that and give it to them. It serves no meaningful purpose to ignore, belittle or dismiss their skill set when involving them in cultivating an effective school climate. Being collegial and building consensus are how you facilitate interaction with Baby Boomers. They do have the knowledge and experience, and their opinions should be taken seriously when making decisions that will affect them.

Communication

Face-time is valued and it allows them to ask questions and feel comfortable with what you want from them, so have meetings. Bring them in on an issue before the decision is made and take advantage of their knowledge and experience regarding that issue.

Recognize Their Contributions

Baby Boomers do not need constant praise. They would rather be recognized only for a job well done. Any monetary contribution or job title recognition is received as a positive exchange of goods for services. Although not necessary for a job completed efficiently and effectively, a $10 gift-card to Starbucks or Target as a show of appreciation once in a while will go a long way in facilitating the Baby Boomers to continue to volunteer and be involved. This is seen as tangible recognition for their knowledge and experience, and lets them know that they are valued. Now I am not advocating that every time a Baby Boomer completes a project that they get a gift-card, but every once in a while it helps. Be cautious! If you give everyone a gift-card, say as a Christmas present, Baby Boomers will not see this as specific validation to their contribution to the success of the school. Whether they admit it or not, they want to feel special in their own special way.

Involvement

Baby Boomers will get involved in any project if you ask or direct them as they value the hierarchy, and they typically will not say "no" to the principal. However, if you can tailor the Baby Boomers' involvement to processes that they find interesting, or are passionate about, then their commitment will be more intense (Table 2.1). By doing this, there is a good indication

Table 2.1 Baby Boomers

Leading Them	What They Need
Communication	Communicate with them in person.
Recognize Their Contributions	Title recognition is important.
Leadership	May be hesitant to share ideas with new staff on how to be successful, but will share more easily if they are in a leadership role.
Involvement	Will be involved if directed, but will be more effective if they have knowledge and experience in what you are asking of them.

that they have a wealth of knowledge and experience with this topic, so selecting them as the "Lead Teacher" in charge of that project or program is also a plus for Baby Boomers.

Moment of Reflection . . .

How many of your teachers fit into the Baby Boomer category? Do these individuals reflect these generalizations? How might this information facilitate your interaction and relationship building with these individuals?

_____

_____

_____

_____

Generation X

Generation Xers make up a larger portion of your teaching population, with 10–20 years in the profession. They are your main "workhorse" that drives the educational process, which continually grows the culture of the building. Before you can influence them and build upon their ability to network with the other generations of teachers, you must first know more about them.

Who Are They?

Gen Xers were born between 1965–1980. They are a generation that wants a balance in their universe. They find personal and professional satisfaction in their work; however, they do not define themselves by their work. Gen Xers pushed for a more balanced lifestyle to match their work ethic. This generation coined the phrase "Work hard, play hard!" They do not define their work day by punching a clock, and often go outside of their "duty day" in order to be prepared for the following day. However, they want flexibility to recoup some of their own time lost in their own work day, or during teacher professional in-service days. Continuous education is assumed as a way to continue to develop and grow as an educator. Gen Xers engage in development that they deem necessary of their time. With that said, they do not like their time wasted on frivolous meetings or trainings that do not meet their individual work needs.

Gen Xers want the important information to be communicated to them in person. They want to know what is important and the time frame that you put on tasks. Other less important information can take place via email. They will prioritize the importance of tasks via email and notify you when they are complete (Hammill, 2005; Karp et al., 2002; Lancaster & Stillman, 2002; Zemke et al., 2000).

Leading Them

In order to be successful in interacting with Gen Xers, as well as cultivating an educational environment conducive for students to grow, the administrator needs to understand how to communicate with them and recognize their contributions. You need to provide leadership they respect and know how to get them involved and committed to the mission and vision of the school.

Assign Gen Xers a task and let them complete it in a manner that they deem appropriate. They do not want to be micro-managed and they find value in showing you unique ways to solve the problem. Resist instructing them how to do a task, and you may be pleasantly surprised by their ingenuity and creative problem-solving processes. Be as flexible as possible with your requests, allowing them to be creative and resourceful. Let them impress you, and make sure to tell them you are impressed with their solutions. They have an entrepreneurial spirit and thrive on being creative, diverse, challenged, and responsible.

Communication

If you have an important task to be completed, meet with Gen Xers in person and be very specific about what you want accomplished, including a time line. Talk about benchmarks toward success and what success looks like. Do not communicate "how" to do a project; they work best at finding solutions to the problem themselves. Just lay out parameters and timetables so that they truly understand the framework for task completion. For less important issues, communicate with them via email, text, etc., and let them prioritize how they accomplish tasks. Give them leeway to accomplish a task, and you will be surprised at their efficiency and effectiveness.

Recognition

Gen Xers want to be recognized for their hard work. They will ask for feedback and need you to provide it to them on a regular basis. They are more entrepreneurial and competitive and want to be recognized in public for their successes. They appreciate tangible rewards, but providing them with "time" may be equally as rewarding. One way to give them this time is to teach one of their classes for a period. It gives them an extra break and lets you receive some experience back in the trenches. You would be amazed at how much renewed respect you will get from the teachers for minimal time in the classroom. They see it as you staying connected to what they experience on a daily basis, and it helps you keep perspective of the current state of the students in the classrooms.

Involvement

Autonomy is important. They want to be involved and committed to education (Table 2.2). They crave opportunities to be autonomous. In fact, if

Table 2.2 Generation Xers

Leading Them	What They Need
Communication	Important issues in person; non-important issues in text or email.
Recognize Their Contributions	They seek public recognition for their accomplishments.
Leadership	They embrace leadership roles and do not want to be micro-managed. Creativity in their processes is important to them.
Involvement	Want to be involved but often want to be autonomous in that involvement. Lack of involvement may cause them to feel unappreciated and look for another school.

they feel that they are not being given enough opportunities to be successful or engage in leadership responsibilities, they will start looking at other schools or professions that will satisfy their need to achieve and grow professionally.

Moment of Reflection . . .

How many of your teachers fit into the Generation X category? Do these individuals reflect these generalizations? How might this information facilitate your interaction and relationship building with these individuals?

_____

_____

_____

_____

Millennials (Generation Y)

Millennials (in the research literature you may also see them referred to as Generation Y) make up the newest addition to our teaching profession. They are new, eager, wide-eyed, and ready to conquer the world. They also don't know what they don't know. Before you can influence them, and build upon their ability to network with the other generations of teachers, you must first know more about them.

Who Are They?

Millennials are the generation who "does not have to be looking at you to hear you." They are constantly multitasking and find it more difficult to concentrate on one thing at a time. They are more in-tune with what you are saying when they can engage in a process that allows their inner voices to be occupied while they concentrate on you (Hammill, 2005; Karp et al., 2002; Lancaster & Stillman, 2002; Zemke et al., 2000).

Leading Them

In order to be successful in your interactions with Millennials, as well as cultivate an educational environment conducive for students to grow, you need to understand how to communicate with them, recognize their contributions, and provide leadership they respect. You also need to know how to get them involved and committed to the mission and vision of the school.

Millennials want responsibility and leadership opportunity but are not going to compete against one another for your acknowledgement. They are social beings who want to include others in the problem-solving process. Get them involved and let them create collaborative processes that will address an issue. Consensus is important, so show them that you value their input. Time is important, so show them you value their time. They are more likely to break the stereotype of "it's always done this way" if they feel like they have some hand in trying to make a process better or more efficient.

Communication

Millennials are multitaskers who see their time as valuable. Face-to-face communication is only necessary for something critical or very important. All other communication can use various forms of technology. Millennials are constantly plugged into technology. Therefore, some of the best ways to communicate with them is through email, text messaging, instant messaging, Facebook, Twitter, etc. (insert any new form of social media that emerges between the time I wrote the book and the time you are reading the book). They will communicate at all hours of the day or night, so it would not be unusual to receive an email at 10:00pm or 5:00am if they have an issue that needs your attention. Work is not a 9:00am–5:00pm job, but rather a function of their daily life.

Recognition

Millennials want instant feedback and recognition. Although all Millennials may not like public acknowledgement, they ALL crave recognition. Feel out the ones who like it in public and give it to them in public. Millennials would rather be recognized as part of an effective team rather than to be singled out, if singling out means that you forget to acknowledge someone's contributions. Due to their social network connections, contributions to education may occur outside of the classroom. They may recruit volunteers or solicit funds for specific activities outside of parents or PTO. Make sure to celebrate them (and all potential community donors) as they will value this recognition.

Involvement

Millennials have an entrepreneurial spirit and work best when you give them a goal and they design the process to attain the goal (Table 2.3). However, they are less competitive and more tolerant of their colleagues. They want to achieve success through collegial support, not competitive edge. Have them form committees or target groups to analyze and address issues or concerns, and let them achieve that together. They will build upon their social network to find solutions and solicit feedback so that they can present back to you the best plan possible. They will only put in their valuable time if they feel the cause is worth it AND that you will value that feedback. They will move onto something else if they feel that you are wasting their time.

Table 2.3 Millennials

Leading Them	What They Need
Communication	Electronic communication is the most direct way to communicate and elicit a response.
Recognize Their Contributions	Want instant feedback and recognition for their accomplishments.
Leadership	They embrace the leadership role but want it to be more consensus building through teamwork. Not big on competing for praise.
Involvement	Are less competitive and build upon their social networks for involvement opportunities.

Moment of Reflection ...

How many of your teachers fit into the Millennials category? Do these individuals reflect these generalizations? How might this information facilitate your interaction and relationship building with these individuals?

_____

_____

_____

_____

_____

Table 2.4 consolidates each section of this chapter into one table for better cross-referencing.

Use Template 2.1 to indicate which category each of your teachers fit in. Do they fall true to the generational splits or are some outliers? Either way, Template 2.1 will assist you in reflecting on each teacher's strengths, and give you an idea on how to begin to meet their needs. A blank template is included as an eResource for your reflective activities.

Table 2.4 Consolidation of the Three Generations of Teachers

Leading Them	Baby Boomers	Generation X	Millennials
Communication	Communicate with them in person.	Important issues in person. Non-important issues in text or email.	Electronic communication is the most direct way to communicate and elicit a response.
Recognize Their Contributions	Title recognition is important.	They seek public recognition for their accomplishments.	Want instant feedback and recognition for their accomplishments.
Leadership	May be hesitant to share ideas with new staff on how to be successful, but will share more easily if they are in a leadership role.	They embrace leadership roles and do not want to be micro-managed. Creativity in their processes is important to them.	They embrace the leadership role but want it to be more consensus building through teamwork. Not big on competing for praise.
Involvement	Will be involved if directed, but will be more effective if they have knowledge and experience in what you are asking of them.	Want to be involved but often want to be autonomous in that involvement. Lack of involvement may cause them to feel unappreciated and look for another school.	Are less competitive and build upon their social networks for involvement opportunities.

Template 2.1 Knowing What Your Teachers Need

Leading Them	Generational Characteristics	Teachers' Names
Communication	Communicate with them in person.	
	Important issues in person; non-important issues in text or email.	
	Electronic communication is the most direct way to communicate and elicit a response.	
Recognize Their Contributions	Title recognition is important.	
	They seek public recognition for their accomplishments.	
	Want instant feedback and recognition for their accomplishments.	
Leadership	May be hesitant to share ideas with new staff on how to be successful, but will share more easily if they are in a leadership role.	
	They embrace leadership roles and do not want to be micro-managed. Creativity in their processes is important to them.	
	They embrace the leadership role but want it to be more consensus building through teamwork. Not big on competing for praise.	
Involvement	Will be involved if directed, but will be more effective if they have knowledge and experience in what you are asking of them.	
	Want to be involved but often want to be autonomous in that involvement. Lack of involvement may cause them to feel unappreciated and look for another school.	
	Are less competitive and build upon their social networks for involvement opportunities.	

A Genuine Leader . . .

A genuine leader takes the time to get to know their staff. They are not cogs in a wheel but rather individual professionals who have a great deal to contribute if they are properly motivated. A genuine leader knows how to lead them, communicate with them, show them recognition, and how to involve them so that they feel fulfilled and valued. By taking the time to get to know your staff, you are taking a significant step towards becoming that genuine leader.

Leadership is only effective if people follow. By knowing your followers, you learn how to best lead them.

CHAPTER TAKEAWAYS

Takeaway Tidbit

● Get to know your staff on a more genuine level.

Takeaway Template

● Knowing What Your Teachers Need Template 2.1 (eResource A).

Takeaway Task

● Complete the Baby Boomer Moment of Reflection.

● Complete the Generation X Moment of Reflection.

● Complete the Millennials Moment of Reflection.

● Complete the Chapter Moment of Reflection.

Moment of Reflection . . .

Reflect on how this information regarding your teachers may guide how you approach them, and solicit their level of support throughout the school year. Did you have "aha" or "oh no" moments? Why?

_____

_____

_____

_____

_____

References

Hammill, G. (2005). *Mixing and managing four generations of employees.* Retrieved October 11, 2014 from http://www.fdu.edu/newspubs/magazine/05ws/generations.htm

Karp, H., Fuller, C., & Sirias, D. (2002). *Bridging the boomer xer gap: Creating authentic teams for high performance at work.* Palo Alto, CA: Davies-Black.

Lancaster, L., & Stillman, D. (2002). *When generations collide: Who they are, why they clash, how to solve the generational puzzle at work.* New York: Harper Collins, Inc.

Myers-Briggs Foundation. (2015). *Myers-Briggs type inventory.* Retrieved October 11, 2015 from http://www.myersbriggs.org/my-mbti-personality-type/mbti-basics/

Personality Profile Solutions. (2015). *Everything DiSC.* Retrieved October 11, 2015 from https://www.discprofile.com/

Zemke, R., Raines, C., & Filipczak, B. (2000). *Generations at work: Managing the clash of veterans, boomers, xers, and nexters in your workplace.* New York: American Management Association.

PART

4 Principles

4 Principles

1. Keep Your Focus on the Child
2. Share Your Vision, NOT Your Brain
3. Understand That Absolute Power Corrupts Absolutely
4. Education Is a "Contact" Sport

Merriam-Webster (2015) defines the word ***principle*** as "A basic truth or theory: An idea that forms the basis of something." The next four chapters outline the 4 principles that form the basic foundation of attitude and atmosphere that you as the genuine school leader must create and facilitate effectively within a school environment.

Step 1
Keep Your Focus on the Child

It must always be first about the child.

Beginning of the Year

As a new administrator getting ready to open the school year at your first building, your stomach is full of butterflies, the excitement that you feel causes you to reflect back to when you were little and anticipating that first day of school. You have a clean, orderly desk, with all of your plans for this school year fresh in your mind, making this year the best that it can be. You made sure the vision and mission statement were up to date, you set goals for yourself and your school, you have conveyed these goals to your teachers, and you believe that they are all on board to making this year better than the last.

For some of you more seasoned veterans, you chuckle a little at this description in part because you remember that feeling and in part because somewhere inside of you are little butterflies that creep in on that first day as well. No matter the school or your experience level, the first day is a fresh start. People expect things to be different, more exciting and positive, but more importantly they expect this year to be more successful than last year. This year will be different. You feel it, the teachers feel it, and in some cases the district office demands it. Nothing is going to stand in your way this year . . . except life.

Then "Life" Happens

First it starts with a small bump. A parent doesn't like a certain teacher, their daughter didn't get placed in the same class as her best friend, their son's schedule doesn't allow him to take both Honors Physics and Calculus 3 this year and now he can't get into Harvard, etc. You tell yourself that this was just a little bump; a hiccup at the very beginning of school. It will certainly pass and you can get back to focusing on the vision, mission, and standards. The first couple of days will probably go well, and in some cases even the first or second week leads you to believe that this year is truly a wonderful departure from the previous year. All students are in their classes learning, all parents are now completely in love with their teachers, nobody is causing a ruckus, fracas, or any other action that has "cus" in it. In fact, it is a good idea to avoid "cussing" altogether.

Then, as if the honeymoon ended, life happens. Students begin to misbehave and you have to deal with it. They are all sent to you so that you can "nip it in the bud early" and get back to that perfect school year. You learn that a certain portion of your students' parents filed for divorce over the summer and now they want to just "stop by" your office to tell you their side of the story and to discuss who has the parental rights. Also, now everything has to go home to both parents as they have restraining orders out against each other and the common ground is the school since the transferring of the student can only occur on your campus. Better yet, they attempt to use you as a pseudo counselor because you listen to them and they want you to believe that they are the "good" parent. So you put the kids in touch with the counselor and you escort the parents off campus in order to get back to those educational standards. As you reach your office, you realize that you haven't visited any classrooms or looked for teachers' enlightening students yet today, and lunch is quickly approaching which means only one thing: lunch duty. You know having a presence in the lunch room helps students to stay seated, eat their food, and clean up after themselves. By now the newness has worn off and the referrals from the cafeteria are on the rise. It is not a question of if you should go in the lunch room, as it is a question of when and for how long.

Not to worry, because today will be different. Today you get to skip lunch duty because the Sheriff just knocked on your door and informed you that there has been a report of drugs and weapons on campus and they have to sweep the cars and lockers with K-9 units. The district approved this about 20 minutes ago but you haven't gotten to your emails yet to read it. Even though this instance doesn't end in any arrests, you brace yourself for the multitude of angry parent phone calls, wondering why there were police on campus, and the presence of dogs frightened their children. The next thing you know the day is over and nothing was completed on your list.

Tomorrow morning you are driving to work telling yourself that today will be better than yesterday. You do your best pep-talk in the rearview mirror while you sip your coffee from a travel mug and put on your best smile. As you pull up to the main school office, you see three facility vehicles in the parking lot and the Director of Facilities standing in your parking spot waiting for you. Apparently, routine maintenance has uncovered mold in three of your classrooms and you have approximately 45 minutes to temporarily reassign those classes for the next 5–7 school days while they remove the mold and refurbish the rooms. The move will have a ripple effect on tardiness, schedule flow, and overall calmness of the day. So you stand there, take a deep breath, and promise yourself that you will get into classrooms tomorrow.

The above examples, which may occur at every level of K-12 education, were just some of the ways in which the school leader can be sidetracked from focusing on the goals and standards of the school. Although these do not occur daily, there are going to be many instances where "life" pulls your focus in other directions. When that occurs, you begin to lose focus on student success. Regardless of your situation, it is easier to lose focus than it is to get it back.

Step 1: Keep Your Focus on the Child

The first step, and foundation principle in developing and maintaining a genuinely positive educational attitude and atmosphere, is simply stated, but often times difficult to do: Keep your focus on the child. Before we jump into this, let us first discuss the need to justify your rationale for making decisions. Any and every decision that you make needs to be appropriately justifiable. Please resist the urge to believe that just because you are the school leader, you can make whatever decision you want and do not owe anyone a reason for your decision. First, it is a false assumption; and second, you need your teachers' trust and respect, neither of which you freely get if you start acting like you don't need to explain the decisions you make.

One time I had a student sent to me from a very upset teacher. This student (we'll call him David) had discovered the right "button" to push that would morph his teacher (who is typically a solid and caring individual) into a red-faced, irrational lunatic. Don't get me wrong, David has spent the greater part of this particular school year perfecting the art of setting his teacher off, so it was no surprise when he arrived at my office. It was also no surprise when the teacher and her grade-level colleagues marched upon my office in protest to my leniency (a day of In-School Suspension was not the level of torture or blood-letting that would have satisfied their need for justice). Again, under normal circumstances, these were kind and good educators, but were caught up in the moment of David's behavior completely irritating them.

What I understood about David is that sending him home was not going to remediate his behavior but rather would be a punitive act that would deny him basic necessities needed to bring about change. David currently is residing in a dilapidated house where the electric and water are shut off on a regular basis. His single-parent mother is doing her best with her limited education and job skill set. The only place that David gets hot meals (breakfast and lunch) is at school. We also frequently provide clean clothes for him to wear when he arrives at school. Suspending this child would do nothing but put this 9-year-old in a potentially dangerous situation with the potential absence of food, water, electric, and parental supervision (For those of you questioning why we didn't notify authorities, let me tell you that yes, we contacted Children Protective Services multiple times, and no, they did not remove him from the home). By keeping him at school, but separating him from the "herd," we can guarantee that he is fed breakfast and lunch, he has access to proper restroom and drinking facilities, he is properly supervised, and he will complete his assignments so as to not fall further behind in his academics. When I explained why suspending David from school was not in HIS best interest, the teachers understood my reasoning. They were not particularly happy with the decision, but they did understand and respect it (the protest ended peacefully).

Every decision you make will be judged, and the media doesn't need your permission to judge you. Nor do parents, teachers, students, community members, etc., need that permission to judge your actions. Often, in lieu of meaningful rationale, people will make up their own reason, which is NEVER flattering towards you. At least if you are open about the process and the meaningful, thoughtful consideration and rationale that went into your decision-making, they may not agree with those decisions, but they may be more likely to respect your decision. No matter the outcome of that decision, it MUST be focused on what is in the best interest of the child.

You must be ready to defend every solution you choose for every situation. Do this by going through a reflection process:

1. State the problem, issue, concern, etc.
2. Identify who is involved in the problem (students, teachers, staff, parents, community stakeholders, etc.).
3. Brainstorm 3–5 possible solutions (start with checking Board policy, law, ethical consideration, etc.).
4. List both positive and negative outcomes for each brainstormed idea (keeping in mind all avenues of reactions and how these potential solutions affect all of those involved).
5. Select the best solution to engage in (always making sure it is what is BEST for students).
6. Roll the solution out to staff to be enacted (being mindful of how it is presented to staff, students, parent, stakeholders, and always give the reason and rationale for the selection of that particular solution).

Use Template 3.1 to walk through this process when you are making decisions about what is best for the child and their overall level of effectiveness on student success. The following example illustrates how to use this template. The middle school counselor just returned from a meeting with the 5th grade transition team from the elementary school that feeds into this middle school. She met with the principal to discuss a particular student by the name of Brandon. Brandon was retained twice in two different school districts before arriving in this school district, where he has been attending 4th and 5th grade. He is currently 13 years old and not receiving any special education services. The retentions were due to habitual absences. The principal used the Keep Focus on the Child template to assist in figuring out the best way to help Brandon be successful.

Template 3.1 Keep Focus on the Child

Problem: – State problem, concern, etc.	– Brandon is a 13-year-old incoming 6th grader. – Retained in Kindergarten and 3rd grade in another district. No clear signs of academic disability. Habitual absences early on at other schools, but better attendance in 5th grade.
Who Is Involved: – Students, teachers, staff, parents, community stakeholders.	– Brandon, Mother, middle school principal, middle school counselor, 5th grade teacher, elementary school principal, school psychologist, district student services supervisor.
Possible Solutions: – Take into account Board policy, law, ethics, etc. – 3 to 5 possible solutions.	1. Leave Brandon where he is at and hope he doesn't drop out (will be a 20-year-old senior). 2. Look at Brandon for a possible academic disability. 3. Socially promote one year to get him closer to his age-appropriate peers (from incoming 6th to incoming 7th grade). 4. Socially promote to age-appropriate peers (from incoming 6th to incoming 8th grade). 5. Put academic interventions in place to support poor academic assessments due to poor attendance in previous years regardless of if he is socially promoted or not.
List Potential Positives/ Negatives of Each Solution: – Try to think of all avenues of reactions. – How do these solutions affect those involved?	1. Would be a 16-year-old 8th grader and a 20-year-old senior (dropout risk). Low / no motivation to grow due to current situation. 2. Brandon's current academic issues appear to be due to previous years' attendance and not capability to achieve academically. 3. Moving from 6th to 7th grade is a jump academically and would need academic interventions in place for support. 4. Moving from 6th to 8th grade is a larger jump academically even with academic interventions in place. 5. Academic interventions could focus on specific strategies, skills, and knowledge acquisition but would require additional adult support.
Selection: – Which solution is BEST for student?	3. Move Brandon from 6th to 7th grade to only be one year behind peers. 5. Put academic interventions in place to focus on specific strategies, skills, and knowledge acquisition.

Roll Out:	In an effort to support Brandon and place him in the best possible position to reach his best potential, including graduating, the committee decided to administratively place him into 7th grade and provide him academic intervention to catch him up as much as possible. Mom has agreed to continue to make sure he is attending school regularly. Prior to the first day of school, the school counselor is going to meet with his incoming 7th grade teaching team to discuss interventions that need to be in place for Brandon. Brandon and his mom will meet with the counselor and teaching team individually prior to the first day of school to talk about his intervention plan.
– How is your solution being rolled out to staff, students, parents, community stakeholders? – Always give reason why the decision was made and its rationale.	

When you look at a situation or issue that requires you to either make a decision or support a decision made by your leadership team or specific teachers, ask yourself the following question: Is this solution going to make me the lead story on the 6 o'clock news? If the answer is no or probably not, it may be acceptable to just mentally file your rationale in your long-term memory and simply make the decision. If you believe that the decision will in fact be news worthy, take the time and effort to detail your decision process, including rationale on why it is the best decision for the child. Be clear to document how this solution will help students learn and be more successful overall. Also, document how this decision will assist students in leaving this school more prepared for the world than when they first entered.

By using the template above to articulate a logical solution for a presenting issue, you can then engage in and most likely win an intelligent debate over your decision. Make sure to clearly communicate these reasons to the audience which the decision affects. When possible, like in the above example, include them in the decision-making process. They deserve to know the reasoning behind your decision and may respect it even if they initially don't agree with it.

A Genuine Leader . . .

A genuine leader must always make it about the child first. Put a sign up in your office to constantly remind you to ask yourself, "Are you making a decision that focuses on what's best for the child?" Better yet, make small signs and distribute them to your teachers to place on their desks as a constant reminder for their decision-making processes. As their decisions ultimately affect you, encourage them to ask themselves these questions before making decisions. At the end of the day, whether that day was great or number 2 on your top 10 list of Worst Days EVER, you have to look at yourself in the mirror and affirm that the decisions that you made today were genuinely focused on the child, and that you did what was best for the child. If your actions affirm these two statements, then find comfort in the fact that on this day, you engaged in genuine leadership and stood firm for those who have no voice. Today you were a child's champion.

CHAPTER TAKEAWAYS

Takeaway Tidbit

- It must always be first about the child.

Takeaway Template

- Keep Focus on the Child Template 3.1 (eResource B).

Takeaway Task

- Use the Keep Focus on the Child template to process through your next situation.
- Complete Moment of Reflection.

Moment of Reflection . . .

Reflect on a time when you had to make a decision about a student (academic or behavioral). Did you genuinely do what was in the best interest of the child? If not, think about how you would have made different decisions if you were truly focused on what's best for the child first, and everything else second.

_____

_____

_____

_____

_____

Reference

Merriam-Webster. (2015). *Principle*. Retrieved on November 15, 2014 from http://www.merriam-webster.com/dictionary/principle

Step 2

Share Your Vision, NOT Your Brain

> Varying voices provide balance and value to decision-making teams.

As school leaders we spend much of the summer planning for the upcoming year. We discuss goals, map out objectives to obtain those goals, and then we set out to achieve them. We build leadership teams that reflect all aspects and departments in our building. Instinctively, we are social creatures who surround ourselves with people who think like us or act like us. So it only makes sense when making decisions about the success of the school to build our leadership team with people who believe, think, and often act like we do. Unfortunately, you may find yourself in a situation where the leadership team only thinks one way and sees things from one perspective. This becomes very dangerous as you may miss certain aspects of a situation that may derail your focus on student success.

The second step, and second foundation principle in developing and maintaining a genuinely positive educational attitude and atmosphere, is developing a team that shares your vision but not your brain. Resist the temptation to create one team, or "brain," where everyone thinks like you. Instead, create one vision where others' thoughts, ideas, and actions, although potentially different, act towards one shared focus.

Research has shown that a common vision is necessary for the effective performance improvement of both students and staff (Capper, Frattura, & Keyes, 2000; Farina & Kotch, 2014; Harvey, Goudvis, & Schroden, 2011; Knapp, Copeland, Ford, Markholt, Milliken, & Talbert, 2003; Lindstrom & Speck, 2004; Scheurich & Skrla, 2003). However, simply embedding a vision on a school website or plaque on the wall does little to drive learning. It is the integration of this vision into the practices and policies of each classroom and grade level that make the difference in student success (Glickman, Gordon, & Ross-Gordon, 2007; Kose, 2011).

Beyond the vision statement, you as the school leader must drive the day-to-day decisions that go into impacting the vision of the school. How you address those decisions, and who you have in place for support, are paramount to student success. Novelist F. Scott Fitzgerald once stated, "The test of a first-rate intelligence is the ability to hold two opposing ideas in the mind at the same time, and still retain the ability to function" (BrainyQuote, 2015). Create a leadership team and include people who think differently than you, but can effectively function within the same shared vision.

When asking for your team's input, suspend your ideas for a moment and listen to their take on a particular situation. Ask yourself, "Is their opinion focused on improving student success? Can their opinion exist within your framework without violating your beliefs of practice?" If the answer is yes to both, then accept their advice and let them spearhead its implementation. No one is more motivated than when they are in charge of making their own idea successful. It does not always have to be your decision, if their suggestion is just as rational and viable. It is also extremely important to value their opinion. Verbalize that value, whether or not you take their advice. Likewise, be able to justify the rationale of whoever's advice you are taking, even if it is your own. Building and maintaining trust and respect with your leadership team is paramount to performing your duties as the school leader.

Remember, a leadership team is a group of educators that you bring into your inner circle to assist in making decisions regarding the educational environment. They are the ones whose advice you rely on. They typically share your vision and have some influence within the larger school community. Who should be involved in that group or how many should meet with you is up to you or your district charter. The point here is when you are selecting this group make sure to surround yourself with people that think differently than you. Avoid stacking it with "yes men" and "yes women." To truly get all sides of a potential situation in order to make the most informed decision possible with the best information at the time, you need diversity in thought, belief, and processes. Dissent can be a powerful spark if it gives you an advantage over the situation.

Selecting a Leadership Team

If you had to pick a group of people to assist in driving the school toward success, reflect on the eight questions listed below and write down a list of names that you feel are trusted keepers of the school culture. These are people who have ingrained themselves in the fabric of the school.

1. Whom do the other teachers listen to?
2. Who takes ownership of the school/culture?
3. Who puts their blood, sweat, and tears into the school so that students are successful?
4. Who can motivate the larger group?
5. Who is the most trusted of the group?
6. Who is a great teacher but is quiet about his or her opinion on what you do, but only implements what he or she is told?
7. Who has been open about dissenting from your ideas or disagrees with the programs you put in place?
8. Who has a negative comment about everything (and freely shares it), but offers no idea on how to fix it?

The above questions are not meant to be all inclusive or only apply to one or a few people. If you answered these honestly, you may have a difficult time narrowing it down to five or six names. Also, do not stop at questions 1–5 and build the team. Questions 6–8 are just as important. For example, the quiet "team player" may have incredibly insightful ideas on how to improve the learning experience within the school but is either too shy, or does not consider themselves valuable contributors to the planning process of the school. I had a teacher one time tell me that she is full of good ideas but when she tries to explain it to the principal, she loses confidence and cannot express it in a meaningful way that makes sense. These teachers often get lost in the crowd, and their valuable contribution is lost with them. Instead of cultivating their knowledge, we allow them to drown in the sea of obscurity.

Two Reasons for Choosing Agitators

You also find teachers who always have a negative comment to make about the programs or processes that you are trying to put into place. There are also the teachers that are more passive-aggressive who will technically implement just enough of your plan to not look like they are being insubordinate, only to proclaim afterwards that your program didn't work in their class. This may be painful to hear so brace yourself . . . , they need to be on your team as well. I say this for two very important reasons. First, when you have a plan or program to positively address an issue, you have thought of all of the reasons why the program will work. Your dissenters have all of the reasons why the program will not work. If you consider some of their reasons before implementation, you will be able to make a more informed decision about the program and be able to modify it, thereby potentially negating the unwanted consequences before its implementation. More knowledge makes you stronger and your decision-making more comprehensive and powerful.

The second reason that you want them on your decision-making team is that you make these teachers part of the solution. They are not going to go back to their classrooms or the teachers' lounge and speak negatively about a program that they helped to develop. Their ownership in the program will alleviate a great deal of "destructive lounge talk" with their colleagues and force them to be a positive force within the educational environment. You will in essence take the energy that they could have used to "sink" your program, and use it to give your program buoyancy.

Take Mr. Done for example. He is on year 28 of his 30-year teaching career, with an established mindset and agenda. He does enough to comply professionally but is more than prepared to put it in "cruise control" for the remaining two years left in education. He freely offered his opinion on the inadequacies of the principal's (Ms. Sands) decision-making abilities, but brings no real viable solutions of his own to solve any issue. He is always more than happy to point out why her decisions weren't going to work to anyone who would listen. So it came as a big surprise to Ms. Sands's leadership team when she invited Mr. Done to join them in resolving an issue that the school was facing.

Kindergartners were having a difficult time getting from the bus to their classrooms on time in the morning. The school campus was arranged in such a way that kindergartners had to walk a significant distance (for them) to get to and from the buses. During our first meeting, for every idea Ms. Sands proposed (additional staff in the hallways, kindergarten teachers at their doors, secretaries corralling them until someone could walk them to their classes, etc.), Mr. Done always had reasons why they weren't going to work. When it had come time to adjourn the meeting, Ms. Sands and Mr. Done both overheard one of her leadership team members whisper to another member, "Why is he here if he's not going to help?" Mr. Done delayed his departure from the conference room, and once the room was cleared, asked her that same question. She told him that she appreciated his input, knowing that he is making sure she looked at these suggestions from all angles so to not miss anything. She caught a hint of a spark of appreciation in his eyes, and she wasn't about to let it be wasted. She went on to say, "I'm excited to hear about any ideas that you'll be bringing to the table at our next meeting. We could really use your experience and advice on this one." He smiled and went to his classroom.

The next morning when Ms. Sands arrived at school, Mr. Done was waiting in the office to speak with her. He said that he couldn't get this issue out of his head and spent the night brainstorming ideas. He proposed that the school establishes a Safety Patrol program, were older students were dropped off by their parents before the buses arrived and they would escort the kindergartners to their classroom. She saw this as an opportunity to be a little "Mr. Done" herself (she couldn't resist). She questioned how he would get parents and students to agree to that on a daily basis. He informed her that since he has spent his entire career at this school and in this community, he knows the parents really well (some were even students of his at one time). He was willing to reach out to some of them and was confident that we could get enough to agree. He also wanted to be the organizer of the Safety Patrols, adding that he had a plan to also use them to cut down on the minor vandalism in the restrooms (what is it about little kids, paper towels in the toilets, and this obsession with emptying the contents of soap dispensers all over the floors?). She validated his ideas and encouraged him to run with it. Mr. Done decreased his level of destructive lounge talk (it never really disappears altogether) and became a more positive contributor to the larger school community.

Let's not kid ourselves: teachers like Mr. Done will be difficult to deal with at first because they will resist any inclusion, as they are not used to that role, so you will have to extend yourself and accommodate them in the beginning. However, when they have accepted their new role, your life will become increasingly easier. They will become more of an advocate and less of an adversary.

When selecting the team that will assist you in driving the vision and cultivating student success, be mindful on how you select members and develop the team's personality. Use Template 4.1 to walk you through this activity so that you take the necessary time to vet your members. Make sure

Template 4.1 Vetting Teachers for Leadership Team

Statement	Reflection		
1. Whom do the other teachers listen to:	Sharon Debbie Jim Heather	Susan Scott Bonnie	
2. Who takes ownership of the school/ culture:	Sharon Debbie Jim Lisa	Susan Scott Bonnie Heather	Rebecca Linda Kathy Charlie
3. Who puts their blood, sweat, and tears into the school so that students are successful:	Sharon Debbie Charlie Lisa	Susan Scott Bonnie Heather	Rebecca Linda Kathy
4. Who can motivate the larger group:	Sharon Debbie Jim Charlie	Susan Scott Bonnie	
5. Who is the most trusted of the group:	Sharon Lisa Scott Bonnie		
6. Who is a great teacher, but is quiet about their opinions, only implementing what they are told:	Bonnie Rebecca Charlie		
7. Who is openly dissenting from your ideas, or disagrees with the programs you put into place:	Jim Heather Debbie		
8. Who has a negative comment about everything (and freely shares it), but offers no idea on how to fix it:	Jim Heather Susan		

to process through all eight questions and not just stop after question 5. While scrolling through this process, continue to ask yourself, "Are you setting your team up to maximize the focus on the students, or are you setting your team up for failure?" The example below illustrates how to use this table.

Once you create a list of names, use Template 4.2 to take the time to truly reflect on how they are connected to you. This may seem futile at first, but do this to accurately get a genuine sense of who they are and how they will be effective in assisting you at comprehensively looking at solutions to current and future situations. Taking the time to do this activity will give you a stronger sense of how each teammate will be able to support your vision of effectively educating all students in your school. The example below illustrates how to use this template.

Template 4.2 Identifying Leadership Team Activity

Teacher Name	How Are They Similar to Me	How Are They Different from Me	Why Do I Value Them
Scott	Motivated, ownership, hard worker.	Brings massive content and curriculum experience to the table.	Understands vision and can drive the group.
Heather	Can motivate teachers to follow her.	Pessimistic at times, looking for the bad in every situation.	Will force me to see both sides of an issue.
Charlie	Motivated, ownership, hard worker.	Quiet / shy but reflective in the process of any situation.	Has great ideas, but needs to be pushed to share.
Lisa	Ownership, hard worker, most trusted.	Task-orientated and great at seeing every detail.	Workhorse who makes sure the details are not overlooked.
Jim	Loves the school and staff.	Openly dissents and has every reason why nothing will work.	Forces me to be creative and mindful of every decision.

A Genuine Leader . . .

Genuine leadership is about trusting in yourself and those around you. It is about embracing the diversity of thought, belief, and processes in order to make the most informed decision about any situation that impacts students. A genuine leader embraces the differences in order to bolster a stronger vision of learning within the school and/or district.

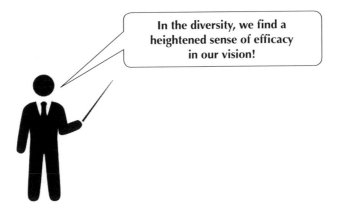

> In the diversity, we find a heightened sense of efficacy in our vision!

CHAPTER TAKEAWAYS

Takeaway Tidbit

- Varying voices provide balance and value to decision-making teams.

Takeaway Template

- Vetting Teachers for Leadership Team Template 4.1 (eResource C).
- Identifying Leadership Team Activity Template 4.2 (eResource D).

Takeaway Tasks

- Complete the Vetting Teachers for Leadership Team Activity.
- Complete the Identifying Leadership Team Activity.
- Complete the Moment of Reflection.

Moment of Reflection . . .

Reflect on who is on your decision-making teams. Do they run the gamut of voices in your school? Do you have a Mr. or Ms. Done? How do you tap them into something positive and constructive both for them and your school building? Reflect on your comfort of allowing a dissenting voice to be at your decision-making table. Can you manage a potential conflict, the dissenting voice, and your leadership team all at the same time? Can you genuinely handle the potential outcomes of some of these interactions?

_____

_____

_____

_____

_____

References

BrainyQuote. (2015). Retrieved October 10, 2015 from http://www. brainyquote.com/quotes/quotes/f/fscottfit100572.html

Capper, C., Frattura, E., & Keyes, M. (2000). *Meeting the needs of students with all abilities: How leaders go beyond inclusion.* Thousand Oaks, CA: Corwin Press.

Farina, C., & Kotch, L. (2014). *A school leader's guide to excellence: Collaborating our way to better schools.* Portsmouth, NH: Heinemann.

Glickman, C., Gordon, E., & Ross-Gordon, J. (2007). *Supervision and instructional leadership: A developmental approach* (8th ed.). Boston: Allyn & Bacon.

Harvey, S., Goudvis, A., & Schroden, A. (2011). *Staff development with a comprehension toolkit: Implementing and sustaining comprehension instruction across the curriculum.* Portsmouth, NH: Heinemann.

Knapp, M., Copeland, M., Ford, B., Markholt, M., Milliken, M., & Talbert, J. (2003). *Leading for learning sourcebook: Concepts and examples.* Seattle, WA: Center for Study of Teaching and Policy.

Kose, B. (2011). Developing a transformative school vision: Lessons from peer-nominated principals. *Education and Urban Society, 43*(2), 119–136.

Lindstrom, P., & Speck, M. (2004). *The principal as professional development leader.* Thousand Oaks, CA: Corwin Press.

Scheurich, J., & Skrla, L. (2003). *Leadership for equity and excellence.* Thousand Oaks, CA: Corwin Press.

Step 3

Understand That Absolute Power Corrupts Absolutely

You do not have to be the expert on everything.

Flashback to your high school freshman or sophomore Language Arts class and you will remember reading great novels like Hemmingway's *Old Man and the Sea* and John Green's *Beowulf*. Side-note: These books are more enjoyable to read as adults, and much better than their movies (no short-cuts). However, one of the most intriguing books that I remember reading was Machiavelli's *The Prince*. Although it was a blueprint to overthrowing a kingdom set in the Renaissance, one message rang loud and clear through-out the book, as well as resonates in many leadership positions today: "Absolute power corrupts absolutely."

The third step, and third foundation principle in developing and main-taining a genuinely positive educational attitude and atmosphere, is the understanding that usurping complete power without the counsel of others could quickly lead to negative outcomes. If people in authority begin to believe that only they are intelligent enough to make the right decisions on everything, they begin to believe that no one else is worthy of leadership. They believe that their hand must be in everything and that any other idea or suggestion from others are not as worthy of their deliberation. This type of leader is making decisions without hearing all of the circumstances sur-rounding the issue, they disregard input from their teachers, and feel that there is no reason to have to rationally explain the decision that they make to their teachers. They tend to parcel out complements and govern with fear rather than engage in genuine collaboration and support. I bet if you think about all of the administrators that you have come in contact with over your lifetime, you can think of one of these types of administrators.

Contrary to popular belief, they didn't wake up one day and decide to be this way. Often they start out just like us. But somewhere along the way they decided that they were the only ones who could make the best decisions for any given situation. At some point they were put into a situation that required them to follow the old saying, "If you want something done right, do it yourself," and it was successful. As more situations arose, they continued with that mantra until they believed that they are the only person who can make the best decision. If this pattern of leadership continues unchecked for a period of time, their leadership looks very autocratic.

Another way that a school leader may turn into an autocratic leader is when they come to the realization that they are responsible for every decision made in the school or district. They may be fearful to share decision-making power when they know that if something goes wrong, they have to answer for it. Then panic sets in and they adopt the mindset of, "If I have to answer for every decision, I must make every decision to protect me." Resist the urge to feel this way, as sharing the decision-making with your teachers and staff will make you a stronger leader.

Transformational Leadership

There are leadership theories that vary along the lines of how to share that power. Transformational leadership, for example, promotes collaboration and sharing leadership with staff (Blase & Blase, 2000; Gill, 2003; Hallinger, 2003; Jung & Sosik, 2002; Leithwood, 1992; Marks & Printy, 2003; Yukl, 1999). Leadership is not distributed from the principal to the teachers; rather, it is shared as teachers accept leadership roles (Leithwood & Jantzi, 2000; Louis & Marks, 1998; Ogawa & Bossert, 1995).

Distributed Leadership

Distributed Leadership (Camburn, Rowan, & Taylor, 2003; Spillane, 2005) is another collaborative leadership style. Distributive Leadership is grounded in the idea that leadership cannot exist in isolation and that in order to maximize the benefits to student learning, leadership must be distributed widely across the organization to those individuals in a position to make the decisions that will elicit the greatest improvement (Elmore, 2000;

Timperley, 2005). Ultimately, the principal maintains control of the school, but utilizes the teachers' respective knowledge, skills, and dispositions by delegating authority and empowering teachers, while continuously cultivating a system conducive to student achievement (Elmore, 2000; Harris, 2005; Spillane, 2005).

Integrated Leadership

A third type of leadership model that promotes a collaborative effort of decision-making is Integrated Leadership (Marks & Printy, 2003). This model recognized the strengths and weaknesses of both distributive and leadership models, and identified pertinent attributes that Marks and Printy believe positively impacted leadership and student success. Regardless of the leadership theory followed, effective principals create an environment where they can tap into the collective intelligence of their staff (Johnson & Kardos, 2005). The principal facilitates a community of educators dedicated to addressing student needs and improving student achievement through collaboration and communication (Blankstein & Noguera, 2004; Burnette, 2002; Garmston, 2006; Hudson, 2005).

Resist the Urge

Principals, by the very traditional definition of their position are often seen as the expert on every facet of the educational environment. Resist the urge to feel like you need to know everything or, more importantly, control everything. With the constant evolving aspect of education, too many things change too quickly for you to be the expert on everything. For example, technology and technological integration into the lives of your students change daily. In fact, research organizations continuously work with educators to make technology a useful learning tool. Trying to be on top of every latest development can drive you mad at times. Canned educational programs are also constantly being development and modified to meet the needs of students. As education learns more about the developmental stages of students, and ways in which to offer interactive curriculum and assessment to improve student success, how we instruct students and deliver instruction will constantly evolve.

District academic standards implementation is one of the largest and most complicated processes to attempt to gain expertise in every facet. Along with this is the continuously evolving standards developed at the federal and state levels. What to teach, when to teach it, and recently how to teach it is a revolving process that can make your head spin. Being an expert in each curricular standard at each grade level and in each subject area is more than a little ambitious.

The following example may help clarify my point. Your secretary walks into your office and tells you the high school science teacher is vomiting in the bathroom and can't return to her class (which starts in two minutes) and you have to go fill in for her this period until they can get a substitute teacher. The lesson today is on understanding the associations of ionic and covalent bonding, including their associative properties both at peak and substandard points of influence. Due to her being sick this morning, she forgot her Teacher's Edition book at home. Is there someone on staff that is more of an expert at this than you, and maybe you could combine the classes for this period? Is there a teacher in that subject area with an open bell that could at least help get the class started in the right direction? The point here is, as the leader you need to be familiar with the standards to perform your duties appropriately, but you do not necessarily need to be the expert in every area. Being familiar is necessary, but being the expert is not necessary if you have people on the staff to whom to delegate that responsibility.

Sharing the decision-making power with teachers allows them to feel valued and supported. Keep in mind that Gen Xers and Millennials crave this type of involvement, and Baby Boomers have a wealth of experience that will contribute to the delegation of responsibility. They are closer to the issues, practice implementing the standards and curriculum on a daily basis, and are using the technology as learning tools in the classroom. They are perfect for these types of teacher leader roles. You have other things that will fill up your plate and delegate where it will be successful for you to do so. Look for the win-win.

One way to keep a situation in perspective, and check your need on whether or not to take absolute control over the situation, is to process through the following points of consideration:

1. What is the problem, issue, concern, situation, etc.?

2. Who has the skills and/or expertise to effectively address this situation?

3. Will I participate in finding and/or implementing the solution?

4. If I delegate, which individual will be in charge of the situation?

5. Will that individual need to create a committee to find a resolution to the situation?

6. If so, who will be in the group?

7. What is the time frame for suggestions to address the situation?

8. Can these meetings be conducted during the teachers' duty times?

9. Does this group require funding or financial resources to find a resolution?

10. How many options are you asking them to present to you for your consideration?

11. Amount of funding needed for each possible solution?

Use Template 5.1 to walk you through this activity so that you process the situation, potentially delegate responsibility, and ultimately address each issue in a manner that brings about effective student success. The example below illustrates how to use this template.

Template 5.1 Problem Assessment and Delegation

Statement	Reflection
Problem:	Trying to get to a 1-to-1 technology ratio in high school, the Superintendent allocated funds for technology purchase. The high school principal needs to decide whether to purchase tablets or laptops.
Who has skill / expertise to address this:	District Technology Coordinator. Classroom teachers at various content and grade levels. Technology teacher.
Will I participate or delegate:	I will delegate the exploration into each of these technology tools.
If delegate, to which individual:	Technology teacher will spearhead committee.

Statement	Reflection
Will that individual lead the group:	Technology teacher will pull together a group of teachers to vet tablets versus laptops. They will consult with Technology Coordinator.
Who is in the group:	Technology Coordinator—Platform infrastructure. Classroom teachers—Curriculum integration using technology. Technology teacher—Student ease of use and integration.
Time frame for suggestions to address the situation:	I would like to have their recommendation within 4 weeks.
Can this be done during duty times:	Possibly.
Does this group require funding:	Not at this time.
Amount of alternative options requested to choose from:	Either tablets or laptops.
Amount of funding needed for each possible solution:	Superintendent funding this.

A Genuine Leader . . .

A genuine leader is more about benevolence than autocracy. By the very nature of your job title, you have to accept responsibility for all decisions made by the individuals you select to lead groups or committees, so spend time building a strong support team who you trust to make the right decisions and who know that you have trust in them. Genuine leadership is about sharing responsibility for student success. However, you must have "big shoulders." When things are going well, share the praise with all of those involved in that process. However, when things go wrong, you as the leader shoulder the criticism. Resist the urge to put the blame on the teachers. You are where the responsibility ultimately resides. By taking the time to create and maintain a culture of shared decision-making, you are taking a significant step towards becoming that genuine leader.

CHAPTER TAKEAWAYS

Takeaway Tidbit

- You do not have to be the expert on everything.

Takeaway Template

- Problem Assessment and Delegation Template 5.1 (eResource E).

Takeaway Tasks

- Practice a Problem Assessment and Delegation Activity.
- Complete the Moment of Reflection.

Moment of Reflection . . .

Reflect on how you approach decision-making. Do you have the need to control everything? Do you genuinely believe that if you want something done right, you have to do it yourself? Are there others in your school that have expertise and experiences beyond yours that add to the positive impact of your building? Are you comfortable with that current situation?

_____

_____

_____

_____

References

Blankstein, A., & Noguera, P. A. (2004). Reclaiming the promise of public education. *School Administrator, 61*(5), 31–34.

Blase, J., & Blase, J. (2000). Effective instructional leadership teachers' perspectives on how principals promote teaching and learning in schools. *Journal of Educational Administration, 38*(2), 130–141.

Burnette, B. (2002). How we formed our community. *Journal of Staff Development, 23*(1), 51–54.

Camburn, E., Rowan, B., & Taylor, J. (2003). Distributed leadership in schools: The case of elementary schools adopting comprehensive school reform models. *Educational Evaluation and Policy Analysis, 25*(4), 347–373.

Elmore, R. (2000). *Building a new structure for school leadership.* Washington, DC: The Albert Shanker Institute.

Garmston, R. (2006). Group wise. *Journal of Staff Development, 27*(1), 73–74.

Gill, R. (2003). Change management—Or change leadership? *Journal of Change Management, 3*(4), 307–318.

Hallinger, P. (2003). Leading educational change: Reflections on the practice of instructional and transformational leadership. *Cambridge Journal of Education, 33*(3), 329–351.

Harris, A. (2005). Leading or misleading? Distributed leadership and school improvement. *Journal of Curriculum Studies, 37*(3), 255–265.

Hudson, J. (2005). Collaboration, inquiry, and reflection: A principal creates a CFG-inspired learning environment. *Educational Horizon, 84*(1), 58–59.

Johnson, S., & Kardos, S. (2005). Bridging the generation gap. *Educational Leadership, 62*(8), 8–14.

Jung, D., & Sosik, J. (2002). Transformational leadership in work groups: The role of empowerment, cohesiveness, and collective-efficacy on perceived group performance. *Small Group Research, 33*(3), 313–336.

Leithwood, K. (1992). The move toward transformational leadership. *Educational Leadership, 49*(5), 8–12.

Leithwood, K., & Jantzi, D. (2000). Principal and teacher leader effects: A replication. *School Leadership and Management, 20*(4), 415–434.

Louis, K., & Marks, H. (1998). Does professional community affect the classroom? *American Journal of Education, 106*(4), 532–575.

Marks, H., & Printy, S. (2003). Principal leadership and school performance: An integration of transformational and instructional leadership. *Educational Administration Quarterly, 39*(3), 370–397.

Ogawa, R., & Bossert, S. (1995). Leadership as an organizational quality. *Educational Administration Quarterly, 31*(2), 224–243.

Spillane, J. (2005). Distributed leadership. *The Educational Forum, 69*(2), 143–150.

Timperley, H. (2005). Distributed leadership: Developing theory from practice. *Journal of Curriculum Studies, 37*(4), 395–420.

Yukl, G. (1999). An evaluation of conceptual weaknesses in transformational and charismatic leadership theories. *Leadership Quarterly, 10*(2), 285–305.

Step 4
Education Is a "Contact" Sport

> Build meaningful relationships with those who come into contact with your school and your students.

Two of the sports that I grew up playing as a kid were football and basketball. I remember being told that football was a contact sport and basketball was a non-contact sport. However, I have very clear memories of being battered and bruised after basketball games and wondering who on earth thought no one made contact in basketball. It was certainly the case of saying one thing, but experiencing another. I believe that this also occurs in schools when we are discussing parent and community involvement.

The fourth step, and fourth foundation principle in developing and maintaining a genuinely positive educational attitude and atmosphere, is the understanding that education is a "contact" sport. It is important that we stress the need to contact and connect with the parents as our primary focus in this section. Parents are a part of the larger community, and may often be your contact and connector to other community stakeholders through their relationships within the community (the community connection piece will be discussed more in Step 6: Building Network Capacity). Reflect on you vision statement, mission statement, and daily ways of practice. If a reporter were to come into your office for an interview and ask if you involve parents, community organizations, and community business leaders actively in your school, your first answer would probably be a quick "Yes." Could you then answer the question of "how" as quickly? This example is how we are saying one thing but experiencing another. For the remainder of this chapter, I will speak more of the parental involvement piece, but it can be generalized to the broader community.

In the era of educational accountability, school leaders focus on instruction and collaboration with teachers in the educational environment, as well as cultivate an environment that promotes and supports parent and stakeholder involvement in the education process. The school and community connection is essential in the learning process of the student. Parental involvement in the education of children has been at the center of the educational movement since the early 19th century in America. Parents and community stakeholders recruited teachers into their towns to provide an education that they deemed necessary for their children to be successful (Berger, 2008; Epstein, 1986; Katz, 1971). Although this involvement has evolved over the years, the essential component of parental involvement has remained the same.

Research Findings around Parental Involvement

Parental involvement in the educational process has been researched heavily over the past few decades. In order to understand the significance on contacting parents and building those connections, it is important to take some time to understand what has been discovered through the plethora of studies. Research findings have suggested that parents and community stakeholders play a significant role in student academic success (Brabeck & Shirley, 2003; Cooper, Crosnoe, Suizzo, & Pituch, 2010; Henderson & Mapp, 2002; Jeynes, 2003, 2007; Leana & Pil, 2006). These positive influences can be measured in tangible outcomes such as higher grades, increased attendance, and overall graduation rates. Likewise, parental involvement also influences student success and well-being with respect to self-esteem, behavior, and positive life goals (Epstein, 2005; Epstein, Sanders, Simon, Salinas, Jansorn, & Van Voorhis, 2002; Fan & Chen, 2001; Herman & Yeh, 1983; Khajehpour, 2011; O'Donnell & Kirkner, 2014).

Parents want a school leader who creates a warm and inviting atmosphere where they feel welcomed to participate as a partner in the educational process. They want a school leader who is open, honest, trustworthy, and who finds value in the involvement of parents. These characteristics influence the level and degree of their involvement, which in turn impacts the level of student achievement (Abrams & Gibbs, 2000; Christenson,

Rounds, & Gorney, 1992; Edwards, 1995; Egan, O'Sullivan, & Wator, 1996; Epstein, 1991; Fan & Chen, 2001; Mawhinney, 2004; Merttens & Vass, 1993; Miretzky, 2004; O'Donnell & Kirkner, 2014; Patterson, 1994).

Parent Attitude and Satisfaction

After a contact is made, it is essential that the school leader develop and maintain a positive connection with parents. Research has shown that this positive connection cultivates a parental attitude and level of enthusiasm towards the school that directly affects student success. Likewise, building and maintaining strong connections with parents can have a positive impact on the education of the parents. When partnering in the education of their children, their attitudes and beliefs about the quality of instruction and effectiveness of teachers improved. They began to seek more education themselves so that they can make a more concerted difference in assisting their children with school-related activities at home (Abrams & Gibbs, 2000; Chavkin & William, 1993; Dauber & Epstein, 1993; Henderson, 1987, 1988).

The school leader must create an educational environment where contacting parents and building connections is a positive expectation at all levels of learning. This environment depends a great deal upon how the school leader develops and maintains teacher perception and attitude of parental involvement. Although the school leader sets the tone of the building, it is the classroom teacher who more directly impacts the involvement process with the parents through those personal contacts and connections.

Teachers' Perception of Parent Involvement

Very often contact to parents and the larger community first comes through the classroom teachers. At the beginning of the school year, teachers are looking to make parents aware of what the parent and the child should expect from their class. This is also an opportunity for teachers to build those connections and relationships with parents through the solicitation of involvement and support.

From the teachers' perspective, parental involvement tends to be seen as either a positive collaborative endeavor or simply as an inconvenience or distraction from their job as the primary educator of students. When teachers feel that their roles are separate from the role of parents (ex: we do the teaching and they do the parenting), contact tends to be less collaborative based. When the schools see children as only students to instruct, they solidify this separation between the product of education and the influence of the family. When teachers and parents have a weak collaborative relationship, teachers rarely requested support or assistance from the parents. In this view, the roles between the teacher and parent are very distinct and the line between them should not be compromised in any way (Anfara & Mertens, 2008; Desimone, Finn-Stevenson, & Henrich, 2000; Epstein, 1986, 1995; Henderson & Mapp, 2002).

When teachers take on a more positive contact approach with parents, they facilitate an environment that supports a collaborative, cooperative, and developing approach on best practices for school improvement. The education of a child is a shared responsibility where parents and teacher partner in the instructional and academic success of students. When schools see children as children and not merely as students, they are likely to see parents and community members as partners in the educational environment (Epstein, 1995; Erginoz, Alikasifoglu, Ercan, Uysal, & Alp, 2015). When teachers and parents have a strong collaborative relationship, teachers frequently request support or assistance from the parents (Epstein, 1986; O'Donnell & Kirkner, 2014). By integrating responsibilities and roles, parents and teachers create a comprehensive learning environment where learning is not limited to occurring only within the school building walls.

When addressing teachers' perceptions about parental involvement, four common themes emerged in the literature:

1. Time Constraints
2. Skill Development
3. Communication
4. Parent Coordinators

Time Constraints

Teachers have always been very protective of their time with students. Developing and implementing curriculum and instruction in a differentiated format can be very demanding, however necessary to assist all students in achieving their highest potential. Teachers who have positive relationships with parents see their involvement as a way to maximize time with specific students in order to increase their effectiveness. Whether support in the classroom as volunteers or support with homework, when parents have the time and skill to support the teacher, the teacher can spend quality time with more struggling students (Becker & Epstein, 1982; Erginoz et al., 2015; O'Donnell & Kirkner, 2014). Conversely, teachers with limited relationships with parents see their involvement as time consuming. Taking the time to train parents on what they need to do in order to support their child's success, or even explaining how to volunteer in their classroom, takes away valuable time from the learning process (Becker & Epstein, 1982). Teachers see this as an unnecessary waste of their most precious commodity: time.

Skill Development

Attached to the issue of time is the teacher's perception that parents lack the knowledge and skills necessary to assist teachers in facilitating student achievement. If the parent were to be involved in the classroom, training has to take place to arm parent volunteers with the knowledge, skills, and methods to assist them in facilitating student achievement (Desimone et al., 2000; Ngwaro, 2012; O'Donnell & Kirkner, 2014). Teachers see taking the time to train and develop parents to be supporters in the classroom, especially if parents cannot commit to a significant consistent volunteer schedule throughout the year, as a waste of valuable time and resources (Becker & Epstein, 1982; Desimone et al., 2000; Epstein, 1995). However, for those teachers who find value in preparing parents by facilitating their knowledge and skill development to assist them in the classroom and at home, they affirm that parents are vital assets in the academic development of the students (Anfara & Mertens, 2008; Desimone et al., 2000; Epstein, 1995; Henderson & Mapp, 2002; Ngwaro, 2012).

Communication

Communication affects the amount of parental involvement in the education of children. For parents to be effective in collaborating with teachers, communication must be a two-way process where teachers and parents are sharing information in a clear and concise manner (Anfara & Mertens, 2008; Cooper et al., 2010; Henderson & Mapp, 2002; O'Donnell & Kirkner, 2014). Whether it is face-to-face, over the telephone, or through informal notes, teachers who actively cultivate parental communication had higher response rates from parents than teachers who did not perceive parent communication as important in the education of the student. When parents and teachers have a healthy communication structure, students will receive common messages about the importance of school and common messages about what it takes to be successful (Cooper et al., 2010; Epstein, 1995; O'Donnell & Kirkner, 2014).

Parent Coordinators

Parent coordinators have shown success in soliciting parental involvement in the school setting (Becker & Epstein, 1982; Ferrara, 2015). Parent coordinators may be teachers with this additional assignment or parents who take on this role in order to increase the involvement of parents in the school. Parent coordinators are dedicated to creating processes and pathways for other parents to feel accepted and valued in the school environment. They develop training programs and coordinate with teachers to fill volunteer gaps that teachers need. When a school has an effective coordinator, the students benefit from the additional adult support in the classroom (Desimone et al., 2000; Becker & Epstein, 1982; Ferrara, 2015). However, if there is not sufficient support for parent coordinators by the teachers or principals, the results will be less effective. Teachers who view parent coordinators as ineffective tend to see this position as unstructured and a waste of financial resources (Becker & Epstein, 1982; Ferrara, 2015).

Teachers' Perceptions of the Principal's Role in Parent Involvement

Teachers' perceptions of effective parental involvement were underscored by the type of educational environment cultivated by the principal. Teachers' who felt that the principal cultivated a school environment conducive for high levels of parental involvement, and whose belief in the level and necessity of parental involvement matched that of their principal, identified their school as positively creating an environment that promotes and welcomes parental input and collaboration (Epstein & Dauber, 1991; Leithwood, Patten, & Jantzi, 2010). Conversely, when there is a discrepancy between the teachers' and principal's beliefs on the level and importance of parental input, the amount of parental input was lower than when the teachers and principal aligned their beliefs (Epstein & Dauber, 1991). Therefore, it is the responsibility of the genuine leader to build a community of common understanding between teachers and parents in order to support teachers' actions in the classroom and facilitate student academic success.

Parents' Perceptions of Opportunity for Involvement

Contact, whether by the school leader or teacher, can only be successful if the parents are receptive to that contact. The purpose of the contact is to establish positive relationships and solicit involvement in the educational life of the student. Much like the teacher perspective, involvement from the parent perspective also sheds light on their role in the educational environment. As with teachers having their perception about parents' ability to assist and support, parents also have their own perception of how teachers include them in the facilitation of their child's learning. Parents want to feel welcome, share in the educational goals of their child, and experience clear communication with their child's teacher (Abrams & Gibbs, 2000; Cowan, 2003; Khajehpour, 2011; Mawhinney, 2004; Miretzky, 2004; Ngwaro, 2012; Zellman & Waterman, 1998).

Research demonstrates that, when schools make a concerted effort to include parents in the education of their child, parents generally felt that the school was welcoming to their involvement. They identified schools as comfortable, well-run, and that the attitude of the teachers and staff were warm and positive. Likewise, schools that seemed to have a focus on a significant parental involvement were identified by the parents as having similar goals as the parents regarding the development of their children (Epstein, 1986; Ferrara, 2015; O'Donnell & Kirkner, 2014).

Clear communication is necessary for parents to understand where their child is performing with respect to their academic development, as well as what they can do to support the teacher and facilitate their child's growth and development both at school and at home (Abrams & Gibbs, 2000; Cooper et al., 2010; Cowan, 2003; Mawhinney, 2004; Miretzky, 2004; Ngwaro, 2012; Zellman & Waterman, 1998). Clear two-way communication allows the teacher to share pertinent knowledge and learning skills so that parents will be able to continue the learning process at home. Parents' communication back to the teacher allows the parents to share if their child is being successful with the current assignments, or if they are struggling to comprehend the curriculum. This supports the teacher in differentiating their instruction to meet the specific child's needs. Clearly, concise communication allows students to receive a consistent, common message that their teacher and their parent are working together to facilitate a positive educational experience (Epstein, 1995; O'Donnell & Kirkner, 2014).

Epstein (1995) found that:

> Parents with children in the classroom of teachers who built parental involvement into their regular teaching practice were more aware of teachers' efforts, received more ideas from teachers, knew more about their child's instructional program, and rated the teachers higher in interpersonal skills and overall teaching quality.
>
> (p. 291)

By teachers including parents in the educating of their child, teachers have a unique opportunity to influence parenting style and to transform ways in which parents approach their child with regard to education (Cooper et al., 2010; Erginoz et al., 2015; Ngwaro, 2012; Zellman & Waterman, 1998).

School Leader's Role

For parents to be involved in the education of their children through parenting, volunteering, communicating, decision-making, and being positive conduits to the larger community, school leaders must establish pathways and opportunities for parents to be interconnected to the school (Berger, 2008;

Epstein, 1995, 1996; Leithwood et al., 2010). Effective parental support involves two-way communication, open collaboration, and meaningful input to the school improvement process. Within a context of community involvement, a school leader must have the knowledge and skills to embrace input from parents and guardians, as well as the sensitivity to cultivate trust relationships that advocate parental involvement in the learning process (Cowan, 2003; Erginoz et al., 2015; O'Donnell & Kirkner, 2014).

Unfortunately, schools often find themselves in positions where they want to engage parents as partners in education, but lack the knowledge to establish and cultivate such a relationship. According to Epstein's (1995) research,

> Just about all teachers and administrators would like to involve families, but many do not know how to go about building positive and productive programs and are consequently fearful about trying. This creates a "rhetoric rut," in which educators are stuck, expressing support for partnerships without taking any action.
>
> (p. 703)

Genuine school leaders must develop these pathways and discover ways in which to engage parents in the learning environment. When they take the initiative and develop educational environments that have a collaborative culture, parental involvement increases at the school (Cooper et al., 2010; Epstein & Dauber, 1991; Leithwood et al., 2010; O'Donnell & Kirkner, 2014). School leaders have the ability and resources to provide training to teachers through staff meetings and workshops on the techniques and the importance of parental involvement both in the classroom and at home as a way to continue the educational learning process for their children (Becker & Epstein, 1982; Khajehpour, 2011; Ngwaro, 2012).

When teachers adopt a positive culture similar to the school leader, and make a conscious effort to build and maintain partnerships with parents, the results are high levels of parental involvement. A genuine leader establishes a culture and environment where teachers find value in parental involvement and empower themselves to build positive partnership with parents, which ultimately have a positive impact on student achievement (Becker & Epstein, 1982; Leithwood et al., 2010).

Clearly, it isn't enough just to contact parents and ask for their involvement. The educational leader must create and maintain an educational environment that cultivates parental involvement. Without such an environment, parents will not become involved in their child's school or be intimidated and withdrawn when they attend school functions (Desimone et al., 2000; Ngwaro, 2012). Without such an environment, parents may face challenges and obstacles, and their efforts may be thwarted as they seek to be involved in processes that support their children's academic achievement within the school learning environment (Becker & Epstein, 1982; Hobbs, Dokecki, Hoover-Dempsey, Moroney, Shayne, & Weeks, 1984; Lightfoot, 1978; Moles, 1982; Ngwaro, 2012). Schools cannot (in appearance and in practice) present itself as unwelcoming or uninviting. Schools bound by rigidly strict controls and aloof hierarchical structures reduce the involvement of parents and community members.

The Contact Is Significant

The robust research and varying caveats of involvement illustrated above lead to the profound understanding that parent contact and their subsequent involvement in the educational process is necessary in growing student success. It demonstrates that by making meaningful contacts and building and maintaining relationships with parents, student achievement, attendance, and graduation rates increase. These positive contacts establish an environment of trust, where the parents and community feel welcomed and involved in the life of the students.

As the educational leader, you must have processes in place to develop and maintain positive contacts, as well as continuously reflect upon the effectiveness of the connections that you have in place. Questions you should be asking yourself and reflecting upon on a regular basis are:

- How are we in contact with students, assisting them in understanding their role in their own learning?
- How are we in contact with parents in order to have them commit to be partners in their child's learning?
- How are we regularly in contact with teachers in their classrooms to support student learning?
- How have we taken steps to reach out to community organizations that can provide programs or resources for our students and their families?

- How are we reaching out to business stakeholders to better understand what they need from us in order to prepare the workforce for the next generation?
- How have we reached out to universities to visit our schools and promote higher educational opportunities so that our students are thinking about their future and what they need to do now in order to get where they want to go?

One example is taking advantage of your school's monthly PTO/PTA meetings. At each monthly meeting, designate time to have conversations with the principal. Parents, community members, and local organizations have a set venue to come and speak with you about anything. Clear your calendar for that evening and stay as long as needed to assist anyone who has come out to meet with you. Also use the PTO venue to involve local organizations, to game plan on how to solicit local support, and to recognize students, teachers, parents, and community for all that they have accomplished for your school. This one avenue should not be considered the be all and end all for stakeholder contact, but rather one of a plethora of ways in which to make these meaningful contacts. Others include attending organizational venues and being open to participating in ways that demonstrate your willingness to support them first. (Once I served time in a dunk tank at the local park to support an organization that focuses on helping children in need. I also served on a Board to build a local library for the school and community to access.)

Use Template 6.1 to make notes and mindfully walk you through your thought processes as you plan contact with students, teachers, parents, and the community. The example below illustrates how to use this template.

As the leader of the school, you are in the best position to cultivate these relationships and develop networks that are beneficial to both your school's and the stakeholders' interests. Also, do not underestimate the networked connections that your teachers have to parents and community stakeholders. Encourage their reaching out as well, and support the connections that they are able to make. Their spouses, family, and/or friends may all be connected to various stakeholders throughout the community. Teachers should be your best-selling asset for the school. Promote and encourage these contacts.

Template 6.1 Contacting Students, Teachers, Parents, and Community

Question	Actions Taken	Actions Needed
How are we in contact with students, assisting them in understanding their role in their own learning?	– Individual academic growth meetings – Progress monitoring – Report cards	– Individualized learning plans – Student presentations of their own learning
How are we in contact with parents in order to have them commit to be partners in their child's learning?	– PTO – Website – Newsletters – Social media	– Set up "talk with the principal" opportunities
How are we regularly in contact with teachers in their classrooms to support student learning?	– Walk-through observations – Email – Team meetings	– Establish data meeting – Solicit what support they need – Open-door policy
How have we taken steps to reach out to community organizations that can provide programs or resources for our students and their families?	– Attend organizational functions – Present to their Board – Solicit partnerships	– Increase number of contacts to established partnerships. – Increase new partnerships
How are we reaching out to business stakeholders to better understand what they need from us in order to prepare the workforce for the next generation?	– Making initial contacts	– Ask them to sit on your advisory board – Invite them in to the high school for discussions on preparing students – Present to students
How have we reached out to universities to visit our schools and promote higher educational opportunities so that our students are thinking about their future and what they need to do now in order to get where they want to go?	– Job / college fairs	– Have professors come in and teach a class – Have career exploring – Have college shadow day

A Genuine Leader . . .

A genuine leader understands the power of true and significant parent and community involvement, and works diligently in making those contacts and connections. Like those of us who do not have 20/20 vision, we often rely on contact lenses to clearly view the world around us. Like contact lenses, sometimes the best way to understand a situation, or have a comprehensive view of your success, is through reflection of what is coming through your contacts. By taking the time to make contacts with students, staff, and the community as a whole, you are taking a significant step towards becoming that genuine leader.

Often times the only way to improve your vision is through contacts

CHAPTER TAKEAWAYS

Takeaway Tidbit

- Build meaningful relationships with those who come into contact with your school and your students.

Takeaway Template

- Contacting Students, Teachers, Parents, and Community Template 6.1 (eResource F).

Takeaway Tasks

- Contacting Students, Teachers, Parents, and Community Activity.
- Completing the Moment of Reflection.

Moment of Reflection . . .

Reflect on the different ways in which you contact students, staff, parents, and the community both inside and outside of the school day. Are those avenues of contact successful? How? Are there better ways to strengthen those contacts? How?

_____

_____

_____

_____

_____

References

Abrams, L., & Gibbs, J. T. (2000). Planning for change: School community collaboration in a full-service elementary school. *Urban Education, 35*(1), 79–103.

Anfara, V. A., Jr., & Mertens, S. (2008). Varieties of parental involvement in schooling. *Middle School Journal, 39*(3), 56–64.

Becker, H. J., & Epstein, J. L. (1982). Parent involvement: A survey of teacher practices. *Elementary School Journal, 83*(2), 85–102.

Berger, E. H. (2008). *Parents as partners in education: Families and schools working together* (7th ed.). Columbus, OH: Merrill.

Brabeck, M., & Shirley, D. (2003). Excellence in schools of education: An oxymoron? *Phi Delta Kappan, 84*(5), 368–372.

Chavkin, N. F., & William, D. L., Jr. (1993). Minority parents and the elementary school: Attitudes and practices. In N. F. Chavkin (Ed.), *Families and communities in a pluralistic society* (pp. 73–83). Albany: State University of New York.

Christenson, S. L., Rounds, T., & Gorney, D. (1992). Family factors and student achievement: An avenue to increase students' success. *School Psychology Quarterly, 7*(3), 178–206.

Cooper, C., Crosnoe, R., Suizzo, M., & Pituch, K. (2010). Poverty, race, and parental involvement during the transition to elementary school. *Journal of Family Issues, 31*(7), 859–883.

Cowan, K. (2003). *The new title I: The changing landscape of accountability.* Tampa, FL: Thompson Publishing Group.

Dauber, S. L., & Epstein, J. L. (1993). Parents' attitudes and practices of involvement in inner-city elementary and middle schools. In N. F. Chavkin (Ed.), *Families and schools in a pluralistic society* (pp. 53–71). Albany: State University of New York.

Desimone, L., Finn-Stevenson, M., & Henrich, C. (2000). Whole school reform in a low-income African American community: The effects of the cozi model on teachers, parents, and students. *Urban Education, 35*(3), 269–323.

Edwards, S. L. (1995). *The effect of parental involvement on academic achievement in elementary urban schools.* (ERIC Document Reproduction Service No.: ED 398–331).

Egan, C. L., O'Sullivan, C., & Wator, V. (1996). *Improving the reading skills of at-risk students.* Unpublished Master's Thesis. St. Xavier University. (ERIC Document Reproduction Service No.: ED 398–545).

Epstein, J. L. (1986). Parents' reactions to teacher practices of parent involvement. *The Elementary School Journal, 86*(3), 277–294.

Epstein, J. L. (1991). School programs and teacher practices of parent involvement in inner-city elementary and middle schools. *Elementary School Journal, 91,* 289–303.

Epstein, J. L. (1995). School/family/community partnerships: Caring for the children we share. *Phi Delta Kappan, 76*(9), 701–712.

Epstein, J. L. (1996). Perspectives and previews on research and policy for school, family, and community partnerships. In A. Booth & J. Dunn (Eds.), *Family-school links: How do they affect educational outcomes?* (pp. 209–246). Mahwah, NJ: Erlbaum.

Epstein, J. L. (2005). Foreword. In E. N. Patrikakou, R. P. Weissberg, S. Redding, & H. J. Walberg (Eds.), *School-family partnerships for children's success* (pp. vii–xi). New York: Teachers College Press.

Epstein, J. L., & Dauber, S. L. (1991). School programs and teacher practices of parental involvement and inner-city elementary and middle schools. *The Elementary School Journal, 91*(3), 289–305.

Epstein, J. L., Sanders, M., Simon, B., Salinas, K. C., Jansorn, N. R., & Van Voorhis, F. L. (2002). *School, family, and community partnerships: Your handbook for action* (2nd ed.). Thousand Oaks, CA: Corwin.

Erginoz, E., Alikasifoglu, A., Ercan, O., Uysal, O., & Alp, Z. (2015). The role of parental, school, and peer factors in adolescent bullying involvement: Results from the Turkish HBSC 2005/2006 study. *Asia-Pacific Journal of Public Health, 27*(2), 1591–1603.

Fan, X. T., & Chen, M. (2001). Parental involvement and students' academic achievement: A meta-analysis. *Educational Psychology Review, 13*(1), 1–22.

Ferrara, M. (2015). Parent involvement facilitators: Unlocking social capital wealth. *School Community Journal, 25*(1), 29–51.

Henderson, A. T. (1987). *The evidence continues to grow: Parental involvement and student achievement.* Columbia, MD: National Committee for Citizens in Education.

Henderson, A. T. (1988). Parents are a school's best friend. *Phi Delta Kappan, 70*(2), 149–153.

Henderson, A. T., & Mapp, K. L. (2002). *A new wave of evidence: The impact of school, family, and community connections on student achievement.* Austin, TX: National Center for Family and Community Connections with Schools.

Herman, J. L., & Yeh, J. P. (1983). Some effects of parent involvement in schools. *The Urban Review, 15*(1), 11–17.

Hobbs, N., Dokecki, P. R., Hoover-Dempsey, K. V., Moroney, R. M., Shayne, M. W., & Weeks, K. H. (1984). *Strengthening families.* San Francisco: Jossey-Bass.

Jeynes, W. (2003). A meta-analysis: The effects of parental involvement in minority children's academic achievement. *Education and Urban Society, 35*(2), 202–218.

Jeynes, W. (2007). The relationship between parental involvement and urban secondary school student academic achievement. *Urban Education, 42*(1), 82–110.

Katz, M. B. (1971). *Class, bureaucracy, and schools: The illusion of educational change.* New York: Praeger.

Khajehpour, M. (2011). Relationship between emotional intelligence, parental involvement and academic performance on high school students. *Procedia – Social and Behavioral Sciences, 15*, 1081–1086.

Leana, C., & Pil, F. (2006). Social capital and organizational performance: Evidence from urban public schools. *Organization Science, 17*(3), 353–366.

Leithwood, K., Patten, S., & Jantzi, D. (2010). Testing a conception of how school leadership influences student learning. *Educational Administration Quarterly, 46*(5), 671–706.

Lightfoot, S. L. (1978). *Worlds apart: Relationships between families and schools.* New York: Basic Books.

Mawhinney, H. (2004). Deliberative democracy in imagined communities: How the power geometry of globalization shapes local leadership praxis. *Educational Administration Quarterly, 40*(2), 192–221.

Merttens, R., & Vass, J. (1993). *Partnerships in maths: Parents and schools, The IMPACTProject.* (ERIC Document Reproduction Service No.: ED 387–355).

Miretzky, D. (2004). The communication requirements of democratic schools: Parent-Teacher perspectives on their relationships. *Teachers College Record, 106*(4), 814–851.

Moles, O. C. (1982). Synthesis of recent research on parent participation in children's education. *Educational Leadership, 40*(2), 44–47.

Ngwaro, J. (2012). Parental involvement in early childhood care and education: Promoting children's sustainable access to early schooling through social-emotional and literacy development. *Southern African Review of Education with Education with Production, 18*(2), 25–40.

O'Donnell, J., & Kirkner, S. (2014). The impact of a collaborative family involvement program on Latino families and children's educational performance. *School Community Journal, 24*(1), 211–234.

Patterson, S. R. (1994). *Increasing parental involvement in grades one, four, and five in a rural elementary school.* Unpublished Ed.D. Dissertation. Nova Southeastern University. (ERIC Document Reproduction Service No.: ED 389–480).

Zellman, G. L., & Waterman, J. M. (1998). Understanding the impact of parent school involvement on children's educational outcomes. *Journal of Educational Research, 91*(6), 370–380.

PART

III

3 Processes

3 Processes

1. Know What You Have / What You Need
2. Building Network Capacity
3. Know Your Role

Merriam-Webster (2015) defines the word **process** as "A series of actions that produce something or that lead to a particular result." The next three chapters outline 3 processes that detail specific actions the genuine leader must engage in to facilitate collaboration and learning within a school environment.

Step 5
Know What You Have / What You Need

In order to cultivate continued student success, you need to know what you have and what you need to facilitate that sustained success.

The fifth step, and first process of action to facilitate genuine collaboration and learning within the educational environment, is identifying what you have and what you need to create and maintain success. In order to know if you are making a difference in the life of a child, you need to take inventory of the tools and resources at your disposal. You need to know what you have at the ready, and what you need to get in order for your teachers to be successful. This isn't a one-time thing that you do at the beginning of your principal career, but rather a process that you engage in for a variety of situations. The examination and re-examination of process implementation is at the foundational core of maintaining high levels of student success. One very structured and powerful method to use in this reflective process is a SWOT analysis (Humphrey, 2005). SWOT is an acronym that stands for Strengths, Weaknesses, Opportunities, and Threats to those opportunities.

STRENGTHS

Whether at the school or district level, a genuine leader needs to know what is in place and working. Although it may start with a simple question of what is working well, being able to answer this can be tricky as some things may be a product of a reaction to the environment and not easy to manipulate. So, let's break this question down into the three components: *programs, materials,* and *support.* Make a list of all of the *programs* successfully occurring in your school that focus on the child. Is it a canned program that is increasing reading comprehension? Is it a dropout prevention program that is keeping students in school and helping them earn their degree? Is it an after-school program designed to support homework and healthy exercise for latchkey students? After making a list of programs, detail why they are being successful. This will help you when funding issues arise and you have to consider possible cuts. Also, this is good to have when the media contacts you, wanting to showcase your school and asks for examples of how the school is helping students be successful. Likewise, make a list of the *materials* that you have that are supporting the success of these programs. Is it technology like Smart Boards, program material like workbooks, or alternative curriculum books? Now list the *support* you are receiving to make these programs successful. Is it teachers, parents, community stakeholders, or some combination of these? Lastly, ask yourself if these programs are doing well enough to continue funding next year.

WEAKNESSES

The next reflective act must be centered on what is not working well in your building. This can be a painful question to ask, but it needs to be answered honestly and openly. Following the components mentioned above (*programs, materials, support*), make a list of all the *programs* currently implemented in your school that you think are either not performing up to the level that you think they should, or not performing at all. After making a list of programs, detail why they are not being as successful as you need them to be. This will help you identify the individual pieces of the program that may be limiting its success. It may also help you in considering whether to invest more time and funding into it, or cut it completely from next year's budget.

Make a list of the *materials* being used in these programs. Are they the most effective materials? Are the materials outdated or insufficient to facilitate a positive change in the program? Now list the *support* these programs are receiving. Do you have the right people in the right positions? Are you understaffed? Basically, is this a weakness due to a "person" issue? Lastly, ask yourself if this program can be saved or if you need to move onto something different. How can you turn this weakness into a strength, or do you cut the program altogether?

OPPORTUNITIES

During the needs assessment of your school or of specific programs, look for the gaps or holes in programs that haven't been addressed. By looking at the strengths and weakness of what is currently in place, you will be able to see opportunities that you can make stronger or more comprehensive. Opportunities are about removing the weakness and maximizing the strengths of each situation.

THREATS

Once you identify the strengths, weaknesses, and opportunities to increase the effectiveness of any program, you now need to identify the threats to implementing these opportunities. What is going to impede its success? What are the threats to the opportunities with the *programs, materials,* and *support?* After you identify possible threats, list ways in which to minimize or overcome those threats.

SWOT in Action

Use Template 7.1 to walk you through this process when you are analyzing a situation or program to better understand its level of effectiveness on student success. The example below illustrates how to use this template.

A school is using a scripted, all-in-one reading program purchased through a vendor to support the English Language Arts (ELA) curriculum. The district purchased this program as a way to increase student reading and ELA skills across grade levels. You have been using it and making sure that it has been implemented with rigor and fidelity, but you have noticed that certain segments of your students are not making the gains that you feel they should be making.

Start the SWOT process by first identifying the reading program's strengths (refer to Template 7.1 for bulleted points). The program is standards-focused, looping back to revisit each standard as it progresses throughout the course. Its lesson delivery is already detailed in a daily pattern of delivery that spans the entire school year. The vendor has a cache of materials and resources linked to each daily lesson.

Next, look at the program's weaknesses. The vendor presents the program as a one-size-fits-all model to solve every student's ELA struggles; however, your experience shows that certain segments of your population are not

Template 7.1 SWOT Analysis

Strengths	– Standards-focused. – Loops back to revisit each standard as it progresses throughout the school year. – Lesson delivery is already detailed in a daily pattern of delivery that spans the entire school year. – The vendor has a cache of materials and resources linked to each daily lesson.
Weaknesses	– One-size-fits-all model not being successful in your school. – Scripted daily lessons hinder creativity and teacher professionalism. – Weekly tests, whether or not students were ready to be assessed. – Overall rigidity of the delivery and pace of the model.
Opportunities	– Use as a foundational curriculum. – Bring in additional resources to meet individual student needs. – Empower teacher professionalism to enrich / remediate learning as needed. – Allow for teacher creativity and ingenuity. – Assessments when the student is ready to demonstrate mastery, and not just "every Friday."
Threats	– Teachers may be comfortable delivering a canned, scripted program. – May stick with the script and daily pacing guide to avoid making a mistake. – Put more reliance on teacher professionalism and their ability to identify additional resources needed to support individual student learning. – New and novice teachers may need additional support. – May need more professional development opportunities.

benefiting from this method of delivery. Teachers are required to follow the scripted daily lessons from cover to cover, not deviating from the script. This doesn't allow teachers to be creative or deviate to the degree necessary to meet the needs of all of the students. In order for the teacher to stay on pace with the daily lessons, it requires them to administer a weekly test. This test needs to be administered regardless of whether the student is ready to be assessed on the mastery of the content being taught. The rigidity and delivery needs to be addressed in order to effectively meet the needs of the individual student.

Once you have identified your strengths and weaknesses, now you must look for opportunities to turn those weaknesses into strengths. Instead of adhering to the rigidity of the scripted program, it may be better to use this as a foundational curriculum. Teachers would begin the lessons using this program, and then enrich or remediate students as needed using additional resources which complement this program. Assessments could be revised, allowing the teacher to assess when the students are ready to demonstrate mastery, rather than on the weekly regiment. These assessments could be constructed to encompass either formative or summative assessments identifying student comprehension of content standards, depending upon the needs of the teacher.

The final phase of the SWOT analysis is analyzing threats to the opportunities and new initiatives you may be considering implementing. Teachers may be comfortable delivering a canned, scripted program. Some teachers may not engage in creativity or ingenuity, but rather stick with the script and daily pacing guide to avoid making a mistake or "not getting to" a portion of the curriculum. This translates to not deviating from the script even though they know students may need something different to grasp the core content. You will need to put more reliance on teacher professionalism and their ability to identify additional resources needed to support individual student learning. This may be especially difficult with new and novice teachers who do not yet have a "full bag of educational tricks" to pull from. Teachers may need professional development in order to better understand how to use the program, and may need additional resources to provide a comprehensive educational approach to student learning.

A Genuine Leader . . .

A genuine leader understands the need to analyze what is and is not working within the educational environment, and engage in a detailed process of reflection that effectively addresses a given situation to bring about an increase in student academic success. As a genuine leader, be mindful when analyzing each piece of SWOT, even if it means that you have to change practices or discontinue an initiative that you implemented if it means that you can maximize student learning by taking a different path. Also, when it is time to do a SWOT analysis, use this opportunity to involve your staff. Gen Xers and Millennials are willing to participate in this type of school improvement process. You can free up more of your time, while simultaneously valuing your teachers in this process. By taking the time to truly analyze your ways of practice, and bringing thoughtful and meaningful reflection to areas of concern, you are taking a significant step towards becoming that genuine leader.

> **When programs and processes come into question, call in the SWOT Team.**

CHAPTER TAKEAWAYS

Takeaway Tidbit

● In order to cultivate continued student success, you need to know what you have and what you need to facilitate that sustained success.

Takeaway Template

● SWOT Analysis Template 7.1 (eResource G).

Takeaway Tasks

● Engage in SWOT Analysis Activities.
● Complete the Moment of Reflection.

Moment of Reflection . . .

Reflect on the needs of your current educational situation. What do you have that is working? What isn't working, and what do you need to make it work? Who are the individuals at the district office who can support you in filling your gaps?

_____

_____

_____

_____

_____

References

Humphrey, Albert. (2005, December). *SWOT analysis for management consulting* (PDF). SRI Alumni Newsletter (SRI International).

Merriam-Webster. (2015). *Process.* Retrieved November 15, 2014 from http://www.merriam-webster.com/dictionary/principle

Step 6
Building Network Capacity

Building network capacity by developing both internal and external networking can lead to positive student outcomes.

There is something true about the saying, "It takes a village to raise a child." Networking is the "building and nurturing of personal and professional relationships to create a system or chain of information, contacts, and support" (de Janasz, Dowd, & Schneider, 2002, p. 192). It is the development of social capital between individuals (parents, teachers, business-owners, etc.) for the purpose of attaining support for student success (Adler & Kwon, 2002; Friar & Eddleston, 2007).

The sixth step, and second process of action to facilitate genuine collaboration and learning within the educational environment, is building network capacity. Building network capacity is redesigning how you develop and maintain the network of individuals and resources necessary to facilitate student success. In Step 4 (Education Is a Contact Sport) you were asked to develop pathways of interaction among the school, students, parents, and larger community. This contact is essential for building networked capacity, as maintaining these positive interactions is essential when establishing and continuing reciprocal relationships with all of the stakeholders.

There are two components in building this network, and you as the educational leader are paramount in bringing those components together in order to fit each situation in a harmonious fashion. As mentioned in Step 2 (Share Your Vision, NOT Your Brain) and Step 4 (Education Is a Contact Sport), you do not have to be the expert in everything and in control of everything. This is why building an effective network is so important.

Internal Network

One component of the larger network, *internal network*, focuses on making those connections with the teachers within your school. This is understanding the process of how you can support them and how they can support you. Teachers also have a plethora of contacts outside of the school system and can cultivate a community of support where they blend their outside network into their school network in order to facilitate student success (Brabeck & Shirley, 2003; Jeynes, 2003, 2007; Leana & Pil, 2006).

One example involves trying to increase the number of volunteers to come and read with struggling students. There was a local business in the area that employed a large number of workers. Multiple attempts by the principal to go through the official channels to elicit volunteers were unsuccessful. Through conversations and positive interactions with one of the teachers, they realized that she attends church with a woman that works in this particular company's Human Resource department. The following Sunday she spoke with her friend at church and by Monday morning the principal had an email from the company wanting to discuss ways in which to have their employees volunteer at the school. The internal network between the principal and the teacher, and her internal network with her friend at church, facilitated a positive connection with a community stakeholder that ultimately academically benefited the students.

External Network

A second component, *external network*, involves the principal's influence on bringing the community stakeholders into the school. This often sounds simple, but takes a concerted effort to do effectively. There are times when you have to fight the urge to make the excuse that if you are out in the community, then you are taking time away from running the school. This is a flawed, short-sided excuse as the benefits that you can go out and bring in may outweigh what you as one person can do alone. It is also important to understand that initially, it may take some of your own free time to establish these relationships. However, if your dedication is toward student success, the time and energy that you show the community and parents goes a long way towards goodwill and collaboration when you need their support (Brabeck & Shirley, 2003; Jeynes, 2003, 2007; Leana & Pil, 2006).

One example of building external network capacity involves agreeing to be on a Development and Construction Board charged with building a local library close to a school. In this particular area, there were many retired individuals who regularly volunteered to work at the libraries throughout the county. Let's call their organization "Friends of the Library." The Friends of the Library, who occupied multiple seats on the Board, had great influence on where the new library was being built. Being the local school administrator, I was asked to sit on the Board and offer my input as needed. This required me to attend meetings during the school day, as well as on selected evenings and weekends. Instead of focusing on the time it would take me out of the school building or eat up my personal time, I recognized this opportunity to tap into this resource and immediately agreed. In the months leading up to the build and opening of the library, I was able to network with the Friends of the Library and build relationships with their governing board. This networking led to them building a partnership with my school, volunteering to read and support math development with my most needy students. It cost me more time and energy initially, but the payoff for student interaction and development was worth it.

Use Template 8.1 to walk you through this process when you are analyzing how to better develop and maintain a strong network capacity, and its overall level of effectiveness on student success. The example below illustrates how to use this template.

Template 8.1 Building Network Capacity

Statement	Reflection
How can they help your students:	**Association of Junior Leagues International** – Provide role models for our youth. – Provide shadowing opportunities. – Provide volunteer opportunities.
What skill sets or resources do they possess that we need:	– Active in public service and community outreach. – Have contacts to a wide variety of businesses and organizations.
How can you help the community:	– Partner with them on community projects. – Identify community needs. – Showcase their accomplishments.

Statement	Reflection
How am I actively going to seek out their interaction:	– Contact the local chapter and set up a meeting.
How do I enter their world and not expect them to just come into mine:	– Meet with their Board. – Offer partnerships to support their community outreach projects.
How can I effectively convey their support when needed:	– Put one of their members on my decision-making team / PTA / Leadership team. – Build strong symbiotic partnerships.
How am I going to make this a win-win for all of us:	– Outline how we can help drive their mission. – Outline how they can help drive our mission.

A Genuine Leader . . .

Genuine leadership involves establishing and growing network capacity by first actively seeking out parent and community stakeholders. You enter their worlds and not just expect them to enter yours. It is better that you make these connections before you need something from them. There are many ways to do this. For instance, you can volunteer to be on a community board (refer to previous example), volunteer your school to partner with community revitalization projects, or by simply attending their children's extracurricular activity events and befriending them. Show that you are interested in their children and in the community outside of what "they" can do for "you."

There always comes a time when you will need their support and expertise for the continued success of your students. Whether it is assisting in passing a levy, support for a new technology lab, or simply volunteers to assist in improving student reading. Help the stakeholders know that their interaction with you is vital to the success of the students. Assist them in seeing the win-win for everyone and celebrate the partnerships at every opportunity. You will be surprised to find that once the relationships are built and networks maintained, the community will be more than happy to be a part of the village raising the child. I can't begin to count how often I've heard, "I always wanted to help the schools, but just didn't know how." It is your responsibility to show them how, as well as maintain that sustained positive relationship. By taking the time to cultivate and maintain both the internal and external network connections, you are taking a significant step towards becoming that genuine leader.

Growing children requires all hands on deck.

CHAPTER TAKEAWAYS

Takeaway Tidbit

- Building network capacity by developing both internal and external networking can lead to positive student outcomes.

Takeaway Template

- Building Network Capacity Template 8.1 (eResource H).

Takeaway Tasks

- Explore how you build network capacity.
- Complete the Moment of Reflection.

Moment of Reflection . . .

Reflect on how you have engaged your teachers and community in network building. How strong are those relationships? Are there any relationships that can elicit community support? Look around your local community. Are there ways to get involved as a representative of the school district, in order to put you in a position to make those connections and build that capacity? Who do you know in the community who could introduce you to the "right" people?

_____

_____

_____

_____

_____

References

Adler, P. S., & Kwon, S. W. (2002). Social capital: Prospects for a new concept. *Academy of Management Review, 27*, 17–40.

Brabeck, M., & Shirley, D. (2003). Excellence in schools of education: An oxymoron? *Phi Delta Kappan, 84*(5), 368–372.

de Janasz, S., Dowd, K. O., & Schneider, B. Z. (2002). *Interpersonal skills in organizations.* New York: McGraw-Hill.

Friar, J., & Eddleston, K. (2007). Making connections for success: A networking exercise. *Journal of Management Education, 31*(1), 104–127.

Jeynes, W. (2003). A meta-analysis: The effects of parental involvement in minority children's academic achievement. *Education and Urban Society, 35*(2), 202–218.

Jeynes, W. (2007). The relationship between parental involvement and urban secondary school student academic achievement. *Urban Education, 42*(1), 82–110.

Leana, C., & Pil, F. (2006). Social capital and organizational performance: Evidence from urban public schools. *Organization Science, 17*(3), 353–366.

Step 7
Know Your Role

Know when to lead, know when to follow, and know when to blend into the background.

The seventh step, and third process of action to facilitate genuine collaboration and learning within the educational environment, is knowing what role to play in any given situation or task. One of the most important concepts to know as a school leader is your role in the building. When asked, most leaders will respond with, "I'm the leader in the building, of course." Well, on paper that may be true, but there are times where the best thing that a school leader can do is step aside and allow others to assume that role. In Step 3 (Understand That Absolute Power Corrupts Absolutely), you learned that you do not have to have all of the answers, but surround yourself with staff that complement each other. Knowing your role will let you know when it is more advantageous for the success of students to lead, to follow, to blend into the background.

Know When to Lead

Knowing when to lead is simple when considering it at the surface level. You went to school to become a leader, you went through internships and practice to demonstrate leadership, and you began the school with your name etched in stone as its leader. In fact, the very moniker of "Principal" came from the conception of "Principal Teacher" for the school building. You are in charge and in the driver's seat. Throughout the school day and school year, you must make decisions that cannot or should not be delegated to a committee or other teacher leaders. Decisions that must be made immediately or which are difficult to make, including those which are mandated from the district office, need to be handled by the principal.

One example is how schools look at data to assess student growth. Most teachers are used to assigning grades to work, averaging the grades each 9-week period, and assigning a letter grade for the report card. The principal (let's call her Ms. Martin), as the instructional leader, needs access to how students are achieving at an individual level, outside of report card grades and standardized state assessments. This includes data needed from students that demonstrate their growth towards mastery of each standard they were being taught. Although the teaching staff (at Elwood High School) understand the need for data analysis, many were not initially comfortable with how to document student growth data. In order to monitor student progress toward these content standards, Ms. Martin required teachers to approach every standard with a pre-assessment to establish a benchmark. She then had them re-assess these standards multiple times throughout the year, being mindful to include review modules within the development of the lesson. Elwood teachers were then instructed to enter this information into an Excel spreadsheet and shared with the principal through an online platform (Google Drive is a good option for this).

Ms. Martin received initial and immediate pushback from the teachers. She was asking them to create assessments, use an interactive spreadsheet to monitor student growth, including using a platform that they were not comfortable with, as a way to share that information with her. Following the tired mantra of "this is how we've always done it" was not good for the students, and not being successful for the staff at Elwood High. Referring back to Step 1: Keep Your Focus on the Child, she made the administrative decision that the staff was going to embark on this new process of monitoring and supporting student academic growth. It was not open for discussion or debate, but a necessary mandate to do what is best for the students.

With the support of professional development and continuous encouragement by Ms. Martin, the initial reluctance led to acceptance, which ultimately led to the embracement of this new process. Teachers, who grasped this concept quickly, began supporting other teachers, including holding after-school classes on how to use Excel, Google Docs, and how to write and use pre-assessment data to monitor student progress. By knowing when and how to lead in this situation, Ms. Martin's staff grew in their abilities, and students benefited from this growth. In situations where staff morale is low or indecision is undermining the vision and mission of the school, a genuine leader steps forward and makes the difficult decisions to keep the educational process moving in a positive direction.

However, genuine leaders also know when to resist the temptation of taking on an authoritarian role all of the time. If the decision doesn't call for immediate and swift action, take the time to cultivate teacher leaders and allow them the opportunity to contribute to the leadership of the building and district. The most difficult decision for a school leader is to know when to step back. Great leaders do not lead everything all of the time (refer back to Step 3 if you want to know how that one turns out). Resist the urge to be in complete control all of the time. So, if you're not leading, then what are you doing? Well, genuine leaders know when to follow.

Know When to Follow

There are times and situations where the decision is best rendered by the very teachers it directly affects. The teacher leader or committee still needs your support in order to have buy-in from the entire staff, so you as the principal engage in "active following." Active following allows you to publicly give your blessing to the committee or teacher leader to make the decision, letting all other staff know that you are going to support their decision, so that the school community will follow their recommendation. You are no longer in the driver's seat, but you are still in the passenger's seat guiding.

One example of knowing when to follow centers on student behavior support. After Mr. Ferris (principal) spent his first year at Evansdale Elementary, he felt that the discipline referral process wasn't as effective as it could be at keeping students on task, or getting them back on task after a moment of lapse in their behavior. What was currently in place was a referral process that sent everyone to the principal for every incident. This process spiraled into a bad situation very quickly. So many students were coming to his office for every big and little offense that he often found himself stuck in his office disciplining students all day. At the same time, teachers were complaining that if he were more visible in the building, students would be acting more appropriately.

Something had to be changed in order to make the process of discipline more effective. Mr. Ferris also knew that sheer dictation of mandated steps would do nothing but have the teachers progress through the steps at light-speed to get the kids to the office, not remedying the situation that it was meant to relieve. He decided that the outcome of a new discipline plan would be best reached and maintained if he took on the role of active follower and cheerleader rather than lead decision-maker. He proposed that a committee needed to be created to look into developing a behavior intervention procedure that all classrooms would follow. Teachers signed up for the Positive Behavior Support Committee and selected the chair of that committee. The committee Chair knew that bombarding the office with students for every minor offense was not acceptable, but they had the freedom to develop a process that would make sense to them.

The Chair scheduled and ran the meetings. The committee represented every grade level and input was given by all so that the end result was acceptable and the new preferred way of practice. Mr. Ferris was there cheering the committee on and supporting consensus. Their final plan was well thought out, involved other teachers, allowed the students cool down periods and alternative places to complete their work, and focused on what was best for the child. The bonus was that it allowed Mr. Ferris to get out into the school more often, touching base with many "frequent fliers" before their behavior escalated to the point where they needed to be moved through the discipline process. This was a win-win, giving teacher ownership and administrative support through the development and implementation of the program.

A genuine leader recognizes the power in letting the teachers spearhead initiatives, while offering public support for their efforts. This process empowers and encourages teachers to step up into leadership roles, while feeling valued by their administrator. Besides knowing when to lead, and follow, there are also times when the most effective thing for you to do as the educational leader is to blend into the background. In other words, genuine leaders know when to get the heck out of the way.

Know When to Blend into the Background

There are instances where you allow the teachers to establish a committee and make decisions regarding their working environment, outside of your direct influence. Nothing promotes community and interconnectivity better then to let teachers see the issue, form a committee, and effectively resolve the issue without the overt need to involve you. It allows the teachers to feel the trust that you put into them, and empowers them to solve their own work-setting issues. This trust builds stronger relationships and interconnectivity in your school community and promotes a win-win philosophy as a way of practice. Teachers quickly learn that they have a significant say in the running of their school, thereby increasing responsibility for their actions and increased ownership of their school.

An example of knowing when to blend into the background centers on student growth and achievement. The teachers at Addison Middle school were trying to find more efficient ways of increasing student growth and achievement. Besides implementing the curriculum with rigor, and progress monitoring student growth, they were not seeing the amount of gains that they wanted in a certain period of time. The teachers were fully vested in coming up with ways in which to increase student learning and teacher understanding of how to more effectively reach students at all grade levels. Addison's Building Leadership Team proposed (and the principal subsequently agreed to) a different way for teachers to come together and support one another. The principal had enough confidence and trust in them that he stepped back and let them run with this new process.

Besides interdepartmental grade-level meetings, the teachers agreed to vertical departmental teaming for the purpose of facilitating a learning continuum within each content area, spanning 6th through 8th grade, in which to draw resources and support to meet each student's individual needs. They chose when to meet, where to meet, what was on the agenda, and how they were going to support each other. Great conversations and implementation around common language, vocabulary acquisition, math fluency, cross-walk visitations, etc., across grade levels came from these meetings. The staff understood their mission, and were engaged in doing their "part" to make the collective "whole" better. They were accountable for each other, and held each other to task. They shared their minutes with the principal as a way to keep him in the loop, but they drove the entire process more effectively than if he had to push them through it. Their buy-in and ownership of the outcomes made all the difference. Leading by blending into the background allows you to privately support the committee, even though a public blessing is not needed as other teachers already buy into their recommendations.

It is important to note that you may start in one area and find yourself switching to another. For example, if teachers are struggling on how to analyze and interpret data, you may initially be in the "Lead" role. Once they become more understanding of the data and comfortable sharing the data, you may be able to turn over the reins to a teacher leader and take on the role of "Follower." Another example may be when teachers wanted to plan a Spring Art show and concert, where you initially felt it was okay to take on the "Blend into the Background" role. As the date began to draw near, and you were seeing that the committee didn't have everything in place to be ready in time for the shows, you are forced to take on that "Leader" role in order to do what's best for kids and your school building.

Use Template 9.1 to walk you through how to make the initial decision on whether you should lead, follow, or blend into the background.

Template 9.1 Lead, Follow, Blend into the Background

Situation: List and reflect upon your situation to decide which style to follow.		
Lead	**Follow**	**Blend into the Background**
You need to make the decision due to either constraints (time, money, district mandates, etc.) or unfavorable pushback (pushing teachers out of their comfort zone, inexperience of staff to make these decisions, etc.) Remember: focus on what's best for kids.	The outcome would be more powerful if you allow some of your teacher leaders to form a committee and address this. Teacher buy-in is crucial, but they need you present supporting and cheerleading them on.	The outcome would be more powerful if you allow some of your teacher leaders to form a committee and address this. Teacher buy-in is crucial and they have the ability to do everything from beginning to end without you needing to be present to add legitimacy to their decision-making ability. So, get out of the way and let them do it.

A Genuine Leader . . .

A genuine leader knows when to lead, follow, or blend into the background. When making the choice not to lead, it is important to realize that you do not lose control or power by allowing others to make those decisions. In fact, it makes you stronger and endears your teachers more to you when you take this approach. Remember genuine leaders do not follow the mantra of, "If you want something done right, do it yourself." Rather, they embrace the concept, "If you want something done right, find the right person for the job." By understanding these processes, and adopting this gradual release model to your personal leadership style, you are taking a significant step towards becoming that genuine leader.

True power and influence comes with giving it away.

CHAPTER TAKEAWAYS

Takeaway Tidbit

- Know when to lead, know when to follow, and know when to blend into the background.

Takeaway Template

- Lead, Follow, Blend into the Background Template 9.1 (eResource I).

Takeaway Tasks

- Use the Lead, Follow, Blend into the Background Activity when the next opportunity arises.
- Complete the Moment of Reflection.

Moment of Reflection . . .

Reflect on decisions made recently. Did you *have* to make them by yourself or did you just *want* to? Were there opportunities to empower teachers to be leaders with you actively following? Are your teachers experienced enough to take the reins and make decisions that positively impact your school? If so, did you let them? If not, what are you doing to get them to the level where they can be that type of teacher leader?

_____

_____

_____

_____

_____

2 Goals

2 Goals

1. Cultivate Student Success
2. Cultivate Teacher Satisfaction

Merriam-Webster (2015) defines the word **goal** as, "Something that one is trying to do or achieve." The next 2 chapters outline 2 significant goals that focus on the essence of academic success and teacher satisfaction. These goals are paramount in sustaining an effective working climate within a genuine school environment.

Step 8

Cultivate Student Success

Grow students through a cycle of learning, filtered by school climate and 21st century skills.

School Climate

In order to understand and cultivate student success, you must first understand the impact that school climate has on that success. Much like the parent involvement concept in chapter 6, a great deal of research has been conducted to better understand how the climate influences student outcomes. It is important to take some time to understand what has been discovered through the plethora of research. The actions and interactions of school leaders and teachers within the educational environment are encompassed within the concept of school climate. Researchers have focused on this concept as a phenomenon that occurs within the school setting that facilitates positive student academic success (Goddard, Sweetland, & Hoy, 2000; Hoy & Hannum, 1997; Hoy & Miskel, 2005; Hulpia, Devos, & Van Keer, 2011; Moolenaar, Daly, & Sleegers, 2010; O'Donnell & White, 2005; Price, 2012; Sebastian & Allensworth, 2012).

Understanding school climate is critical in the process of improving student achievement, as the health of the school environment impacts the students' abilities to demonstrate academic success. It is also equally critical to understand that the school leader has a direct impact on the school climate (Blase & Blase, 2002; Cotton, 2003; Gurr, 1997; Hallinger, 2003; Hallinger & Heck, 1998; Haynes, Emmons, & Ben-Avie, 1997; Howard, Howell, & Brainard, 1987; Hoy, 1990; Hoy & Clover, 1986; Hoy &

Hannum, 1997; Hoy & Miskel, 2005; Hoy, Smith, & Sweetland, 2002; Hulpia et al., 2011; Sebastian & Allensworth, 2012; Sergiovanni, 2000).

Schools are perceived as communities where the principal plays an important role in facilitating the movement and direction of that community. Within these educational environments, perceptions of the climate drive the day-to-day direction of the school. In order to better understand the relationship between school climate and student academic success, it is necessary to have a clear definition of the characteristics that comprise school climate. School climate has been defined as a set of distinguishable actions and behaviors within the school that accentuate its unique properties. These properties shape teacher perception of the work environment (Hoy & Clover, 1986; Hoy & Hannum, 1997; Hoy & Miskel, 2005). School climate has also been defined as an atmosphere of attitudes and emotional bonding, specifically teacher attitude and perceptions of collegial work (Howard et al., 1987; Hoy et al., 2002). This includes intimate professional socializations with colleagues, as well as a sense of community support for each other.

My personal favorite definition, because I feel that it encompasses the essence of the school climate concept, is the "Enduring quality of the school environment that is experienced by participants, affects their behavior, and is based on their collective perceptions of behavior in schools" (Hoy, 1990, p. 152). It is prudent, however, to mark a clear distinction between school climate and school culture. Often used interchangeably in the literature, it is important to understand the difference in order to have a better understanding of the construct of school climate.

Climate versus Culture

When school climate and school culture are not clearly differentiated, it becomes more difficult to understand how each one affects student academic success. Although climate and culture at some level both deal with morale, ways of practice, and organizational success, they are, in fact, distinct constructs describing the educational environment (Glisson, 2007; Van Houtte, 2005). Van Houtte (2005) identifies the difference between climate and culture using the concept of time. Culture is steeped in heritage and ways of practice that span across tenures of school leaders. It survives disruptions and maintains the long-term vision and direction of the school. Climate is more focused on how teachers and the principal currently feel about their school. It typically is short in duration and is flexible to fit the current needs of the students, school, and community. Climate, over time, does affect the culture of the school (Glisson, 2000, 2007; Glisson & Green, 2006; Hobby, 2004). Van Houtte further delineated between climate and culture when he stated, "culture concerns values, meanings and beliefs, while climate concerns perceptions of those values, meanings and beliefs" (p. 75). Ultimately, culture is about how things occur in the school environment, whereas climate is about how school leaders and teachers perceive those occurrences influencing their ability to be successful at increasing student academic success (Glisson, 2000, 2007; Glisson & Green, 2006; Lindahl, 2006; Schein, 1993; Schneider, Brief, & Guzzo, 1996; Schneider & Hall, 1972).

School Leader's Influence on School Climate

School climate is directly impacted by the leadership practices of the principal. The principal's ability to motivate the staff and to facilitate the development of quality instructional practices impacts the success of the students (Howard et al., 1987; Hoy & Hoy, 2003; Hulpia et al., 2011; Marzano, Waters, & McNulty, 2005; Price, 2012). School leaders are responsible for maintaining a climate that is collegial, interactive, and focused on supporting the teacher and student throughout the educational process. By setting the tone of the building, school leaders cultivate teacher morale, parent partnerships, and professional collegiality, which in turn influences the delivery of instruction to students (Hoy & Clover, 1986; Hoy et al., 2002; Moolenaar et al., 2010; Price, 2012; Witcher, 1993). High teacher morale increases job satisfaction and sense of school cohesiveness and pride.

School climate is not a stagnant concept but, rather, a continuously changing condition that needs to be monitored and cultivated (Hoy & Hoy, 2003). The school leader monitors the climate and adjusts processes and practices in order to keep the environment healthy and flourishing. This type of environment lends itself to teachers and staff wanting to come to work and engage with students and parents in a positive and productive manner.

When school leaders take the time and mindfully attend to the individual needs of their staff, and facilitate knowledge and skill development within the complex community of educators, there is a positive effect on school climate (Hulpia et al., 2011; Kelley, Thornton, & Daugherty, 2005; Moolenaar et al., 2010; Sebastian & Allensworth, 2012). When principals engage in processes where teachers are empowered to influence the aspects of instruction, collaboration, and support, they increase their ability to have a positive impact on school climate and student success (Hulpia et al., 2011; Leithwood, 1992; Pepper & Thomas, 2002). Whether school leaders take a prominent role in controlling the development of a positive environment or facilitate a work environment where teachers and staff are empowered and participating in cultivating a healthy work atmosphere, a healthy educational atmosphere allows teachers to positively impact student academic success.

School Climate Influence on Teacher and Student Success

Healthy school climates are associated with higher teacher job satisfaction and positive student outcomes. Positive climates exude warmth, belonging, and collegiality. This type of atmosphere promotes a safe, trusting, and meaningful environment that encourages academic and personal growth and development (Hulpia et al., 2011; Hoy, Tarter, & Bliss, 1990; Maninger & Powell, 2007; Moolenaar et al., 2010; Price, 2012; Sebastian & Allensworth, 2012).

Positive school climates allow teachers to build what Goddard et al. (2000) identify as academic emphasis. Academic emphasis is where teachers believe students have the capability to achieve and provide academic instruction that supports that belief. Standards are high and learning is differentiated to support the students' individual needs so that students work diligently to succeed and meet their teacher's expectations. Goddard et al. identified that a climate where academic emphasis flourishes supports not only teachers individually but also the school community as a whole. School leaders are responsible for this focus on academic emphasis by maintaining an environment where teachers can provide that support to students.

Use Template 10.1 to walk you through this reflective process on how you as the school leader cultivate a healthy school climate. Make sure to

Template 10.1 Cultivating School Climate

	What You Are Doing Now to Cultivate a Healthy Climate	What You Need to Create / Maintain / Enhance to Cultivate a Healthy Climate
Teacher Morale	– Treat everyone as professionals – Celebrate accomplishments	– Activity or function outside of school (bowling, softball, etc.)
Professional Collegiality	– Committees – Cultivating team meetings – Share decision-making	– Encourage cross-grade level / cross-content interaction
Facilitate Skill Development	– In-school professional development – District-wide professional development	– Survey teachers on their needs
Opportunities for Teacher Empowerment	– Spearheading committees – Shared decision-making power on certain issues	– Find out teachers' interests and areas of expertise for future support
Partnerships	– PTA / PTO – Churches (food distribution) – Some local businesses	– Expand to larger businesses – Civic organizations

detail what you have in place that is supporting a healthy climate, and brainstorm ideas on what procedures to put into place to help grow those areas of needs. The example above illustrates how to use this template.

The robust research provides a compelling argument that the foundation of student success is rooted in the school leader's ability to develop and maintain a healthy school climate. Therefore, in order to influence student academic outcomes, the genuine leader must engage in actions and processes that promote a positive school climate. With that being said, we will turn our focus now onto Step 8: Cultivate Student Success, and the school leader's influence on that success.

Step 8: Cultivate Student Success

The eighth step, and first goal of sustaining an effective working climate within a genuine school environment, is cultivating student success. Student success must be the primary goal of all educational leaders. I use the term "success" very deliberately. It is often interchanged with the term "achievement" rather haphazardly when the definitions of both words are relatively different. Achievement is often associated with student scores on some type of standardized and/or norm-referenced assessment that students are required to complete on an annual basis. Limiting student success to a single assessment is short-minded and flawed. Student success is a daily, on-going journey that everyone in the building engages in for the purpose of benefiting each individual child. A standardized assessment is just one way of demonstrating student success. It is no more or less important than student engagement, demonstration of skills, and displaying cultivated talents; all of which can be reasonably assessed on a report card.

For the administrator, student success is the result of a well-planned and purposeful execution of curriculum and instruction based on the state standards within the daily school setting. Administrators support the teachers' cultivation of student success by facilitating the cycle of learning.

There are a plethora of cycles of student improvement and learning. Academic institutions promote these types of cycles. For example, Kent State University (2014) has a 6-step cycle: Identify Goals, Identify Objectives, Specify Approaches, Specify Measures, Evaluate and Share Results, and Make Changes. The University of Wisconsin-Superior (2014) uses a 5-step loop: Identify Learning Goals and Outcomes, Provide Learning Opportunities, Assess Student Learning, Reflect Upon the Results, and Improve Teaching and Learning. A quick online search also reveals a variety of teacher blogs and "for-profit" organization sites containing these types of improvement cycles. Wikispaces (2014) identifies a 5-step cycle they call the "5 E's": Explore, Explain, Extend, Engage, and Evaluate. The Johnson Education Group (2014) offers professional development training (for a cost) on their 5-step model: Lesson Planning, Instruction, Formative Assessment, Summative Assessment, and Analyzing Student and Teacher Performance. Regardless of which cycle of learning model you choose to follow, make sure that it at least contains the following four primary components: *Identify, Implement, Assess,* and *Adjust.*

Identify

In order to plan learning for each student, teachers need to identify their students' current level of achievement. States have already outlined expected student achievement benchmarks at the end of each grade level, so school leaders and teachers need to know where students are academically starting the year. Think of it as a mini SWOT analysis for each student. What do they know, what do they not know, what do they need to know by the end of this year, and how are we going to get them there?

For example, Cherry Grove School District uses an individual online assessment called MAP (Measurement of Academic Progress, 2016). It is an online assessment that assists in determining a student's instructional level in both Reading and Math. Each elementary school assesses students three times per year: fall, winter, and spring. The fall assessment identifies their instructional score and predicts the expected amount of growth for each child. Attainment of those growth projections are determined by their spring assessment. Both the Reading and Math assessment outcomes detail areas of strength and concerns so that the teacher can identify each student's individual needs and design an action plan of implementation for targeting those needs. As stated at the beginning of this chapter, it is never a good idea to only rely on one assessment to determine student instructional levels. Besides classroom curricular assessments, Cherry Grove schools also engage in DIBELS (2016) and aimsweb (2016) testing in order to provide a more comprehensive view of each student's instructional level. Although the above mentioned programs are purchased for this specific purpose, you can achieve similar results by reviewing teacher-created pre-assessments and identifying levels of mastery within the context of the content.

Along with identifying where the students are starting, it is also necessary to identify the plan that teachers must put into place, in order to move them to the pre-identified benchmark standards. Keep in mind that some of the students will need more than a year's growth to make it to those benchmarks. Their goal should be modified to get them as close as possible so that next year they will be even closer to the updated benchmark standards.

Ms. Brown, Noah's 3rd grade Reading teacher, examined Noah's MAP report, which indicated that he scored a 174 on his fall assessment. The report also indicated that he is projected to score a 188 on his spring assessment. Ms. Brown knows that she needs to design a plan to move Noah at least 9 points to demonstrate a year's growth. This includes a plan that addresses key ideas and details, informational texts, and vocabulary acquisition and use. Once Noah's Reading abilities and gaps are identified, the next step is the implementation of an educational plan to address his needs.

Implement

The implementation of curriculum through instructional processes is paramount to student success. Teachers are charged with differentiating instruction in order to address the learning needs of all students. Ms. Brown knows that Noah's score of 174 is equal to that of someone scoring at the beginning of 2nd grade. Instead of starting him on the 3rd grade curriculum, she differentiates it to reach back to where he is currently achieving. Her goal will be to grow him as much as possible over this school year so that the deficit gap closes as he moves into 4th grade. She will need support from her 2nd grade colleagues and current teammates to move Noah in an efficient and effective direction. She will also need support from her principal to accomplish this task.

School leaders must make sure that teachers are up-to-date on the best professional practices in varying the delivery of instruction, as well as providing the necessary resources that allow teachers to focus more on individual student success. Your role as the educational leader is to remove the visible, and often invisible, barriers that limit teacher effectiveness. This includes providing a plethora of support that you will read about in Step 9. The takeaway here is make sure teachers have the resources and processes in place to implement instruction in a differentiated manner, including the ability to reach beyond their current grade level or subject area assignment to reach the student's beginning level of learning.

Assess

The third component of the learning cycle is assessment. Assessment comes in many forms and is not relegated to only standardized tests. Assessment of student learning should be occurring on a daily basis. Two of the generally accepted forms of assessment are formative and summative assessment. Formative assessment is a type of assessment that occurs more frequently. It can be as formal as a quiz or as informal as raising hands or oral responses to questions. As new concepts or skills are introduced, the teacher is consistently monitoring student understanding through formative assessment. It is making sure the student grasped one concept before moving to the next concept. To use an outdated, yet universally understood example, it is more like worksheets and quizzes, not chapter tests. When a teacher creates a lesson plan, they identify objectives for the day. Formative assessment is used to identify if they mastered those objectives successfully.

For example, when walking through a class the other day, I observed a lesson where the teacher would pause momentarily and ask the students to demonstrate their level of understanding the lesson. The students held up the fingers from 1 to 4 (1 = totally lost, to 4 – they could teach it to someone in the class) She was then able to ask specific questions, partner students up with each other, and pull a group to the back table for more intense remediation and review.

Another example occurred in a math class where each student had a dry-erase marker and small white slate. The teacher would pose the problem on the board and the students had to write the answers on their white slates. He held a clipboard where he kept running records of their progress. By using the slates, he could easily see who was struggling with the concept and made note of it on his clipboard. He made adjustments to the lesson in real time and supported each student's acquisition of knowledge. During work time, he pulled small groups back to his table to process where they were having difficulty in the computation of the problem.

Summative assessments are more formal assessments of student knowledge and application (there is a whole Bloom's Taxonomy that needs to be addressed, but not in this book). This is the type of assessment used by teachers when they are ready to move to the next concept or chapter. Summative assessment is the evaluation of student learning once the larger concept has been taught. It is the monitoring of the students' understanding of the weekly or concept objectives. Summative assessments may also include standardized assessments. It is the "big picture" of learning, rather than the daily quick checks for understanding.

Continuing the example of Noah from above, the MAP and DIBELS assessments allowed Ms. Brown to implement summative assessments multiple times throughout the school year, outside of chapter or content specific assessment. These assessments allowed her to keep track of Noah's progress and assisted her in better predicting how he would perform on the state mandated tests.

Adjust

So what happens when we are not successful in facilitating learning for all students? Do we merely chalk it up to, "Well, we taught it so they should have learned it," and move into the next concept or chapter? Of course not! Once we identify what students need, implement the delivery of instruction, and assess its success, if learning did not occur for some of our students, we need to adjust our delivery of instruction and remediate the concept(s). We are here to grow all students, and through the differentiation of instruction we will meet that expectation. There are various learning styles and ways to deliver instruction. It is our responsibility to support teachers in finding the instructional styles that our students need in order to grasp the knowledge and be successful. Make sure there are processes in place to adjust the teachers' deliveries of instruction to compensate for students who were not successful during their initial exposure to the lesson.

Use Template 10.2 to walk you through how teachers are engaging in the cycle of learning to increase their effectiveness on facilitating student success. You may want to spend some significant time on analyzing your school's climate and culture as well. The effectiveness of the cycle of learning will be directly related to the relative "health" of the school building in terms of climate and culture.

It is not enough for us to "try"! Parents have entrusted us with their most precious treasures, and we must not fail in the education of our future citizens. Failure only occurs if we choose not to continually adjust our

Template 10.2 Cycle of Learning

Cycle of Learning	Essential Questions
Identify	What resources or processes do you have in place to identify student learning needs / gaps in learning?
Implement	What resources, strategies, curriculum, processes, etc., are teachers using to drive the instructional process? What are teachers doing to grow student success?
Assess	What assessments are your teachers using to measure student understanding of the concepts being taught (include both formative and summative)? Do they need more professional development on how to use these more effectively?
Adjust	How are teachers adjusting their delivery of instruction to meet the needs of those students who did not initially master the concept of the lesson? Are they doing something different or re-teaching the same lesson and expecting different results?

delivery practices until we facilitate student success. As a genuine leader, you must ensure that your teachers have all of the necessary resources available to adjust their strategies and differentiate instruction. This includes being a resource yourself if the need arises. Genuine leaders also make a concerted effort to understand their school's climate and culture, taking care to cultivate a healthy learning environment for their students.

Before I move into the next section in this chapter, I want to say that I am not necessarily endorsing MAP, DIBELS, or aimsweb (I have no stock in the companies and get no kickback for mentioning their names). I mention them strictly as potential resources used to assist in the progress monitoring of students.

Integrating 21st Century Learning Skills into the Learning Cycle

As we prepare, deliver, and analyze daily lessons using a student learning cycle, it is equally as important that we are weaving 21st century learning skills within this framework. When preparing students to successfully compete in the labor market of the 21st century, demands are placed on school leaders to make sure students are beings exposed to and mastering the necessary 21st century skills. The Partnership for 21st Century Skills (2007) released a comprehensive analysis of skills needed to be obtained by students in order to effectively enter and be successful in the 21st century workforce. The skill sets were categorized into four areas: core subjects and interdisciplinary themes, learning and innovation skills, information-media and technology skills, and life and career skills.

Core Subjects and Interdisciplinary Themes

Skills adopted in the 21st century must be rooted firmly in core curricular areas (The Partnership, 2007). Research has shown that when students attain mastery of in-depth knowledge associated with such content as mathematics, reading, and sciences, they can more easily transfer this knowledge to "real world" situations (Bransford, Brown, & Cocking, 2000).

Interdisciplinary themes encompass "global awareness, financial, economic, business and entrepreneurial literacy, and civic literacy" (The Partnership web-page, 2007). Having the knowledge to effectively operate within these particular areas in combination with the skill set to innovatively understand diverse perspectives will prepare students to be competitive in a global economy (Dale, 2005; Leonard, 1998; Spring, 2008). School leaders must ensure both academic rigor and relevance are occurring in the classroom. Along with this, they need to make sure that teachers are presenting these core curricular courses with a focus on innovation and diversity.

Learning and Innovation Skills

Within learning and innovation skills, students need to master critical thinking and problem-solving skills, develop creativity and innovation, and perfect their communication and collaboration skills (Spring, 2008; The Partnership, 2007). The U.S. Department of Labor (1991) identified thinking skills as one of the dominant skills needed for successful workplace assimilation. Critical thinking skills describe a focused and purposeful process, usually for the purpose of solving an issue or achieving a goal. Problem solving has also benefited from a shift in practice. Although the process to solve a problem may be the same (Canter, 2004), there is a renewed focus on how individuals collaborate when given access to the internet and software that allows for the exchange of ideas to flow more easily. From blogging to open-source programs, individuals can connect on a global platform, allowing them the opportunity to collaborate in a more diverse and meaningful manner (Friedman, 2008).

In today's globally competitive market, creativity and innovation are dominant attributes that will facilitate success in the workplace (Borg & Mayo, 2005; Friedman, 2008; Spring, 2008). Sternberg (2007) stated that individuals need to have:

> creative skills, to produce a vision for how they intend to make the world a better place for everyone; analytical intellectual skills, to assess their vision and those of others; practical intellectual skills, to carry out their vision and persuade people of its value; and wisdom, to ensure that their vision is not a selfish one.
>
> (p. 11)

With the use of modern technologies, students must learn how to communicate and collaborate in unique ways. Oral and written communication skills, both in face-to-face interactions and through internet capabilities, are desired attributes in new hires (Friedman, 2008; Sternberg, 2007). Moreover, mastering communication and collaborative skills has been shown to produce an increase in students' academic achievement, social skills, and positive self-esteem (Johnson & Johnson, 1989).

Information-Media and Technology Skills

The 21st century skills associated with information, media, and technology are information literacy, media literacy, and information communication and technology literacy (Borg & Mayo, 2005; Spring, 2008; The Partnership, 2007). Information literacy involves understanding what information is important and how to access this information (Borg & Mayo, 2005; Spring, 2008; Stoer & Magalhaes, 2004). With information doubling every 5.5 years, and technology information doubling every two years (Jukes, 2007), students must have the knowledge and skills necessary to access multiple modes of information sources simultaneously in order to stay competitive.

Multiple forms of media are present in today's culture. Students will not only take information from these sources, but also add information to these media outlets (Friedman, 2008). Media literacy allows the individual to:

> Access information from a variety of sources, analyze and explore how messages are "constructed" whether print, verbal, visual or multi-media, evaluate media's explicit and implicit messages against one's own ethical, moral and/or democratic principles, express or create their own messages using a variety of media tools, and participate in a global media culture.
> (Center for Media Literacy, 2007, web-page)

Information communication and technology literacy uses "digital technology, communications tools, and/or networks to access, manage, integrate, evaluate, and create information in order to function in a knowledge society" (ETS, 2001, p. 2). It combines technological prowess with information resources to provide a more efficient and effective way to provide services or resources for the workplace.

Life and Career Skills

Life and career skills encapsulate the knowledge, skills, and dispositions necessary for students to successfully enter and effectively compete in the 21st century workforce. They must possess attributes of flexibility and adaptability, as well as be innovative and self-directed. They need social and cultural skills to take on responsibility and leadership roles in order to be productive and accountable for their contribution to the workplace (Borg & Mayo, 2005; Spring, 2008; The Partnership, 2007). These attributes are not only desired by employers, but also are associated with a higher level of income over the professional lifetime of the individual (Olson, 2007).

Summing Up 21st Century Learning Skills

Under the realization that schools in the 21st century are preparing individuals to connect and compete on a global market (Borg & Mayo, 2005; Dale, 2005; Friedman, 2008; Spring, 2008; Stoer & Magalhaes, 2004), school leaders must use knowledge gained from the past (Hallinger, 2003; Leithwood, 1992; Marks & Printy, 2003; Printy & Marks, 2006), solicit support from appropriate stakeholders (Blackmore, 2002; Goldfarb & Grinberg, 2002; Kumashiro, 2000; Riehl, 2000), traverse inequitable educational gaps (De Gregorio & Lee, 2002; Park, 1996; Psacharopoulos, Morley, Fiszbein, Lee, & Wood, 1995; Ram, 1984), and develop and maintain an environment that focuses on skills that are both rigorous and relevant (Dale, 2005; Spring, 2008; The Partnership, 2007) to produce functioning world citizens. Taking on such an endeavor as an individual school leader could prove to be overwhelming and most likely ineffective. However, if you keep in mind Step 3 (Understanding That Absolute Power Corrupts Absolutely) and Step 4 (Education Is a Contact Sport), as well as Step 6 (Building Network Capacity) and Step 7 (Know Your Role), you will be able to effectively facilitate student acquisition of 21st century skills within a collaborative framework. This allows you as the school leader to establish and maintain a solid foundation of sustained student success.

Template 10.3 Integration of 21st Century Learning Skills

	What You Are Doing Now to Integrate 21st Century Learning Skills into the Content Areas	What You Need to Create / Maintain / Enhance to Integrate 21st Century Learning Skills into the Content Areas
Core Subjects and Interdisciplinary Themes		
Learning and Innovation Skills		
Information-Media and Technology Skills		
Life and Career Skills		

Use Template 10.3 to reflect on how you as the school leader are promoting the integration of 21st century learning skills into the curricular content areas. Make sure to detail what you have in place that is supporting that integration, and brainstorm ideas on what procedures to put into place to help grow those areas of need.

A Genuine Leader . . .

A genuine leader understands that in order to evoke significant student success, they must first create and maintain a climate and culture conducive to bring about that success. Likewise, a genuine leader understands that in order to grow students academically, teachers need to be engaging in a cycle of learning that tracks student development and provides teachers with valuable information to make informed decisions about each specific child. This includes establishing an environment where 21st century learning is valued and implemented. By taking the time to create and cultivate this type of learning environment, you are taking a significant step towards becoming that genuine leader.

Students are our most precious national treasure. What we do to them, we do to ourselves.

CHAPTER TAKEAWAYS

Takeaway Tidbit

- Grow students through a cycle of learning, filtered by school climate and 21st century skills.

Takeaway Templates

- Cultivating School Climate Template 10.1 (eResource J).
- Cycle of Learning Template 10.2 (eResource K).
- Integration of 21st Century Learning Skills Template 10.3 (eResource L).

Takeaway Tasks

- Complete the Cultivating School Climate Activity.
- Reflect on the Cycle of Learning Process.
- Complete the Integration of 21st Century Learning Skills Activity.
- Complete the Moment of Reflection.

Moment of Reflection . . .

Reflect on the climate of your building. How does it feed or starve student success? How might you increase the level of student success by implementing and analyzing the cycle of learning in a consistent manner? How might 21st century learning skills enhance your ability as a genuine leader to grow students and staff toward a higher academic level?

_____

_____

_____

_____

_____

References

Aimsweb. (2016). *aimsweb Pearson.* Retrieved January 20, 2016 from http://www.aimsweb.com/

Blackmore, J. (2002). Leadership for socially just schooling: More substance and less style in high-risk, low trust times? *Journal of School Leadership, 12*(2), 198–222.

Blase, J., & Blase, J. (2002). Teachers' perceptions of principals' instructional leadership and implications. *Leadership and Policy in Schools, 1*(3), 256–264.

Borg, C., & Mayo, P. (2005). The EU memorandum on lifelong learning. Old wine in new bottles? *Globalisation, Societies & Education, 3*(2), 203–225.

Bransford, J., Brown, A., & Cocking, R. (2000). *How people learn: Brain, mind, experience, and school.* Washington, DC: National Academy Press.

Canter, A. (2004). A problem-solving model for improving student achievement. *Principal Leadership: High School Edition, 5*(4), 11–15.

Center for Media Literacy. (2007). *The heart of media literacy is informed inquiry.* Retrieved April 12, 2010 from http://www.medialit.org./about_cml.html#vision

Cotton, K. (2003). *Principals and student achievement: What the research says.* Alexandria, VA: Association for Supervision and Curriculum Development.

Dale, R. (2005). Globalisation, knowledge economy and comparative education. *Comparative Education, 41*(2), 117–149.

De Gregorio, J., & Lee, J. (2002). Education and income inequality: New evidence from cross-country data. *The Review of Income and Wealth, 48*(3), 395–416.

DIBELS. (2016). *Dynamic Indicators of Basic Early Literacy Skills.* Retrieved January 20, 2016 from https://dibels.org/dibels.html

Educational Testing Service. (2001). *Digital transformations: A framework for ICT literacy. A report of the international ICT literacy panel.* Princeton, NJ: ETS. Retrieved April 5, 2010 from http://www.ets.org/Media/Tests/Information_and_Communication_Technology_Literacy/ictreport.pdf

Friedman, T. (2008). *Open-courseware celebration at MIT.* Retrieved April 5, 2010 from http://www.youtube.com/watch?v=EcE2ufqtzyk

Glisson, C. (2000). Organizational climate and culture. In R. Patti (Ed.), *The handbook of social welfare management* (pp. 195–218). Thousand Oaks, CA: Sage.

Glisson, C. (2007). Assessing and changing organizational culture and climate for effective services. *Research on Social Work Practice, 17*(6), 736–747.

Glisson, C., & Green, P. (2006). The effects of organizational culture and climate on the access to mental health care in child welfare and juvenile justice systems. *Administration and Policy in Mental Health, 33*(4), 433–448.

Goddard, R., Sweetland, S., & Hoy, W. (2000). Academic emphasis of urban elementary schools and student achievement in reading and mathematics: A multilevel study. *Education Administration Quarterly, 36*(5), 683–702.

Goldfarb, K., & Grinberg, J. (2002). Leadership for social justice: Authentic participation in the case of a community center in Caracas, Venezuela. *Journal of School Leadership, 12*, 157–173.

Gurr, D. (1997). *Principal leadership: What does it do, what does it look like?* Melbourne Australia: Department of Educational Policy and Management, University of Melbourne.

Hallinger, P. (2003). Leading educational change: Reflections on the practice of instructional and transformational leadership. *Cambridge Journal of Education, 33*(3), 329–351.

Hallinger, P., & Heck, R. H. (1998). Exploring the principal's contribution to school effectiveness: 1980–1995. *School Effectiveness and School Improvement, 9,* 157–191.

Haynes, N. M., Emmons, C., & Ben-Avie, M. (1997). School climate as a factor in student adjustment and achievement. *Journal of Educational and Psychological Consultation, 8*(3), 321–329.

Hobby, R. (2004). *A culture for learning: An investigation into the values and beliefs associated with effective schools.* Retrieved August 4, 2010 from http://www.schools-of-ambition.org/sofa/files/Culture%20for%20Learning.pdf

Howard, E., Howell, B., & Brainard, E. (1987). *Handbook for conducting school climate improvement projects.* Bloomington, IN: The Phi Kappa Educational Foundation.

Hoy, A., & Hoy, W. (2003). *Instructional leadership: A learning-centered guide.* Boston: Allyn and Bacon.

Hoy, W. K. (1990). Organizational climate and culture: A conceptual analysis of the school workplace. *Journal of Educational & Psychological Consultation, 1*(2), 149–168.

Hoy, W. K., & Clover, I. R. (1986). Elementary school climate: A revision of the OCDQ. *Educational Administration Quarterly, 22*(1), 93–110.

Hoy, W., & Hannum, J. (1997). Middle school climate: An empirical assessment of organizational health and student achievement. *Educational Administration Quarterly, 33*(3), 290–311.

Hoy, W., & Miskel, C. (2005). *Educational administration: Theory, research, and practice.* Boston: McGraw-Hill Co.

Hoy, W., Smith, P., & Sweetland, S. (2002). The development of the organizational climate index for high schools: Its measure and relationship to faculty trust. *High School Journal, 86*(2), 38–50.

Hoy, W., Tarter, C., & Bliss, J. (1990, August). Organizational climate, school health, and effectiveness: A comparative analysis. *Educational Administration Quarterly, 26*(3), 260–279.

Hulpia, H., Devos, G., & Van Keer, H. (2011). The relationship between school leadership from a distributed perspective and teachers' organizational commitment: Examining the source of the leadership function. *Educational Administrative Quarterly, 47*(5), 728–771.

Johnson, D., & Johnson, R. (1989). *Cooperation and competition: Theory and research.* Edina, MN: Interaction Book Company.

Johnson Education Group. (2014). *Teaching cycle.* Retrieved December 12, 2014 from http://www.johnsoneducationgroupinc.com/services.php

Jukes, I. (2007). *From Gutenberg to Gates to Google: Education for an on-line world.* Retrieved April 10, 2010 from http://www.ibo.org/ibap/conference/documents/IanJukes-FromGutenbergtoGatestoGoogleandBeyond1.pdf

Kelley, R., Thornton, B., & Daugherty, R. (2005). Relationships between measures of leadership and school climate. *Education, 126*(1), 17–25.

Kent State University. (2014). *Six steps for continuous improvement of student learning.* Retrieved December 12, 2014 from http://explore.kent.edu/aa/guide/fulltext.html#Resources

Kumashiro, K. (2000). Toward a theory of anti-oppressive education. *Review of Educational Research, 70*(1), 25–53.

Leithwood, K. (1992). The move toward transformational leadership. *Educational Leadership, 49*(5), 8–12.

Leonard, D. (1998). *The wellsprings of knowledge: Building and sustaining the sources of innovation.* Boston: Harvard Business School Press.

Lindahl, R. (2006). *The role of organizational climate and culture in the school improvement process: A review of the knowledge base.* Retrieved December 11, 2010 from http://cnx.org/content/m13465/1.1/

Maninger, R., & Powell, D. (2007, March). The Lincoln Middle School paradigm shift: A case study. *Journal of Educational Leadership, 10*(1), 22–31.

Marks, H., & Printy, S. (2003). Principal leadership and school performance: An integration of transformational and instructional leadership. *Educational Administration Quarterly, 39*(3), 370–397.

Marzano, R., Waters, T., & McNulty, B. (2005). *School leadership that works: From research to results.* Alexandria, VA: Association for Supervision and Curriculum Development.

Measurement of Academic Progress. (2016). Retrieved January 20, 2016 from https://www.nwea.org/

Merriam-Webster. (2015). *Goal.* Retrieved on November 15, 2014 from http://www.merriam-webster.com/dictionary/principle

Moolenaar, D., Daly, A., & Sleegers, P. (2010). Occupying the principal position: Examining relationships between transformational leadership, social network position, and schools' innovative climate. *Educational Administration Quarterly, 46*(5), 623–670.

O'Donnell, R., & White, G. (2005). Within the accountability era: Principals' instructional leadership behaviors and student achievement. *NASSP Bulletin, 89*(645), 56–71.

Olson, L. (2007). What does ready mean? In ready for what? Preparing students for college, careers, and life after high school. *Education Week, 26*(40), 7–12.

Park, K. (1996). Educational expansion and educational inequality on income distribution. *Economics of Education Review, 15*(1), 51–58.

The Partnership for 21st Century Skills. (2007). *The intellectual and policy foundations of the 21st century skills framework.* Retrieved April 12, 2010 from http://www.p21.org/route21/index.php?option=com_content&view=article&id=219&Itemid=293

Pepper, K., & Thomas, L. H. (2002). Making a change: The effects of the leadership role on school climate. *Learning Environments Research, 5*(2), 155–166.

Price, H. (2012). Principal-teacher interactions: How effective relationships shape principal and teacher attitudes. *Educational Administrative Quarterly, 48*(1), 39–85.

Printy, S., & Marks, H. (2006). Shared leadership for teacher and student learning. *Theory into Practice, 45*(2), 125–132.

Psacharopoulos, G., Morley, S., Fiszbein, A., Lee, H., & Wood, W. (1995). Poverty and income inequality in Latin America during the 1980s. *Review of Income and Wealth, 41*(3), 245–264.

Ram, R. (1984). Population increase, economic growth, educational inequality, and income distribution: Some recent evidence. *Journal of Development Economics, 14*, 419–428.

Riehl, C. (2000). The principal's role in creating inclusive schools for diverse students: A review of normative, empirical, and critical literature on the practice of educational administration. *Review of Educational Research, 70*(1), 55–81.

Schein, E. (1993). On dialogue, culture, and organizational learning. *Organizational Dynamics, 22*(2), 40–51.

Schneider, B., Brief, A. P., & Guzzo, R. A. (1996). Creating a climate and culture for sustainable organizational change. *Organizational Development, 24*, 7–19.

Schneider, B., & Hall, D. (1972). Toward specifying the concept of work climate: A study of Roman Catholic diocesan priests. *Journal of Applied Psychology, 56*(6), 447–455.

Sebastian, J., & Allensworth, E. (2012). The influence of principal leadership on classroom instruction and student learning: A study of mediated pathways to learning. *Educational Administration Quarterly, 48*(4), 626–663.

Sergiovanni, T. (2000). *The lifeworld of leadership: Creating culture, community, and personal meaning in our schools.* San Francisco: Jossey-Bass.

Spring, J. (2008). Research on globalization and education. *Review of Educational Research, 78*(2), 330–363.

Sternberg. R. (2007). Finding students who are wise, practical, and creative. *The Chronicle of Higher Education, 53*(44), 11–12.

Stoer, S., & Magalhaes, A. (2004). Education, knowledge and the network society. *Globalization, Societies & Education, 2*(3), 319–335.

University of Wisconsin-Superior. (2014). *Cycle of assessment.* Retrieved December 12, 2014 from https://www.uwsuper.edu/assessment/slo/index.cfm

U.S. Department of Labor. (1991). *What work requires of schools: A SCANS report for America 2000.* Retrieved March 31, 2010 form http://wdr.doleta.gov/SCANS/whatwork/whatwork.pdf

Van Houtte, M. (2005, March). Climate or culture? A plea for conceptual clarity in school effectiveness research. *School Effectiveness & School Improvement, 16*(1), 71–89.

Wikispaces. (2014). *5 e's learning cycle.* Retrieved December 12, 2014 from http://smartideas.wikispaces.com/Activity+Four

Witcher, A. E. (1993). Assessing school climate: An important step for enhancing school quality. *NASSP Bulletin, 77*(554), 1–5.

Step 9
Cultivate Teacher Satisfaction

Being open, honest, accessible, and compassionate to the needs of the teachers increases their satisfaction, which has a direct impact on student success.

The Wallace Foundation commissioned Karen Seashore Louis, Kenneth Leithwood, Kyla Wahlstrom, and Stephen Anderson to engage in a 6-year study, which included 180 schools in 43 school districts in 9 states. The results of their research were published in a report titled, "Investigating the Links to Improved Student Learning" (2010). Of the multiple findings, two stood out as particularly significant in facilitating goals of student success. One, the only person that influences student success more than the principal is the classroom teacher. Two, the administrator has a significant influence on the teachers' work environment, which in turn has a strong influence on the teachers' abilities to facilitate student success. In other words, the administrator's influence on student success is mediated through the teacher. As teachers are more satisfied with their work setting and environment, which is the direct result of the principal's influence, student success increases. Therefore, if the administrator is focused on student success then they must cultivate a positive, interactive, and collegial working environment for the teachers. With this being the case, teacher satisfaction within their working environment becomes very important to the success of the educational organization.

The ninth step, and second goal of sustaining an effective working climate within a genuine school environment, is cultivating teacher satisfaction. Teacher satisfaction perpetuates a level of respect, trust, empowerment, and support that motivates teachers to perform at high levels of effectiveness and facilitates overall enjoyment in the job. The school leader has a significant direct influence on teacher satisfaction and must effectively address the needs of the teachers in order to facilitate a positive environment (Gimbert & Fultz, 2009). Listed below are 10 general points in which school leaders can specifically engage in increasing teacher satisfaction within the learning environment. Although this is not an all-encompassing list, it is a good starting point to begin cultivating this type of environment.

Teachers Want to Be Visited Often in the Classroom and Receive Feedback on Their Performance

Teachers value the engagement in best practices as a way to facilitate student learning and need support and/or affirmation that what they are doing is acceptable. They want their leaders to be both positive and critical as they learn and grow professionally. They need guidance, advice, and empowerment through both acceptance and praise (Angelle, 2006; Gimbert & Fultz, 2009; Renwick, 2007; Richards, 2004; Ruder, 2005).

Teachers Want Their Administrator to Be Conscientious of Their Workload

It is important, especially for novice teachers, to feel success early in their profession. School leaders, who set them up for success by providing them with less challenging assignments and fewer duties outside of the classroom, increase that initial success. For more experienced teachers, administrators being conscientious of their workload provides more opportunities for them to master their craft without feeling overwhelmed. Taking steps such as these allow teachers to spend more time developing their teaching skills and overall impact on students (Davis & Bloom, 1998; Gimbert & Fultz, 2009; Menchaca, 2003; Walsdorf & Lynn, 2002).

Teachers Want Administrators to Have an Open-Door Policy

Trust, honesty, and fairness are important to teachers and solidify satisfaction within the learning environment (Bodycott, Walker, & Lee Chi Kin, 2001; Kardos, Johnson, Peske, Kauffman, & Liu, 2001). Oftentimes dealing with parents, students, and colleagues place undue stress upon the teacher. As the school leader, be there to support them through these times, encourage them to ask questions, and help them understand that you find more strength and confidence in their ability when they ask for help, rather than struggle blindly in how to reach students (Brock & Grady, 2007; Gimbert & Fultz, 2009; Mauer & Zimmerman, 2000).

Administrators Facilitate the Teachers' Navigation through the Climate and Culture of the School

School leaders must be aware that teachers are better prepared to assimilate and become productive members of the educational community when they understand the school's climate and become part of the collaborative culture for learning. This includes the process of teacher cooperation, classification of workload responsibilities, time management, and the implementation of subject matter. The collective responsibility of the school must be clearly defined and consistently implemented by the administrator (Gimbert & Fultz, 2009; McKerrow, 1996; Watkins, 2005; Wood, 2005).

Teachers Want Administrators to Clearly Define Their Roles and Expectations of Their Performance

Teacher satisfaction increases when school leaders clearly state the roles and expectations that they have for teachers. Not only do they need to know expectations for delivering instruction, but also expectations around other assigned job duties, professional standards, student interaction, and content development (Brock & Grady, 2007; Gimbert & Fultz, 2009; McKerrow, 1996; Melton, 2007; Smith, Morrow, & Gray, 1999). Providing clarity of expectations before the year starts, and reinforced throughout the year, gives teachers a framework for success, thereby increasing their job satisfaction.

Teachers Want Administrators to Facilitate Access to the Curriculum and Guide Them on How to Assess Learning

The process of designing the instructional plan is a combination of art and strategy. Teachers need to feel confident in their understanding of curriculum standards so that they can develop and deliver a standards-based lesson (Quinn & Andrews, 2004), as well as how to assess student learning through data driven instruction (Cheng & Cheung, 2004; Davis & Bloom, 1998; Gimbert & Fultz, 2009; Melton, 2007). School leaders need to provide avenues for teachers to obtain and implement curricular practices at high levels of understanding and effectiveness.

Teachers Want Administrators to Ensure That They Have the Tools and Resources for Success

School leaders must acquire the supplies and materials necessary for teachers to do their job effectively (Davis & Bloom, 1998; Gimbert & Fultz, 2009; McCann, Johannessen, & Ricca, 2005; Quinn & Andrews, 2004). New teachers will not inherently know which staff to go to in order to get the appropriate supplies. As the school leader, you support them through this process, and assist them in making the proper contacts.

Teachers Need Guidance on How to Use Data to Guide Classroom Instruction

The school leader facilitates professional development to cultivate sophisticated data analysis skills in their teachers in order to train them on how to use data effectively. They also need to be taught how to extract data from assessment tools to examine the needs of diverse learners and struggling students (Brendle-Corum & Haynes, 2004; Gimbert & Fultz, 2009).

Teachers Need Mentoring and Collaboration

School leaders need to implement a comprehensive mentoring program that promotes a strong instructional development component, which includes aspects of building teacher confidence and empowerment (Brock & Grady, 2007; Gimbert & Fultz, 2009; Johnson & Kardos, 2005; McCann et al., 2005; Melton, 2007; Quinn & Andrews, 2004; Ruder, 2005; Stansbury, 2001). Likewise, a strong collaborative component is necessary for teacher and program development (Renwick, 2007; Wayne, Youngs, & Fleischman, 2005; Wong, 2004).

Administrators Cultivate a Culture and Value in Continual Opportunities to Learn Professionally, Both Individually and Collectively

Teacher needs may align or vary widely from their colleagues. Having individual professional development opportunities allow teacher needs to be addressed on an individual basis, and are essential for their success and satisfaction (Amoroso, 2005; Black, 2004; DePaul, 2005; Ganser, 2002; Gimbert & Fultz, 2009).

Use Template 11.1 to walk you through how you as the school leader are promoting teacher satisfaction within the educational environment. Make sure to detail what you have in place that is supporting that satisfaction, and brainstorm ideas on what you need to put into place to help grow those areas of needs. The next example illustrates how to use this template.

Template 11.1 Cultivating Teacher Satisfaction

How often do you visit teacher classrooms and give feedback on their performance?
– Informal walk-throughs monthly. – Formal observations twice a year.
How are you conscientious of their workload?
– Number of students in the classroom, including student level of intensity. – Job duties and committee placement.
How have you initiated / maintained / supported an open-door policy?
– At school an hour before it starts and an hour after it ends. – Teachers know they can text me 24 hours a day.
How have you navigated teachers through the culture of the school environment?
– New teachers—give history of school and identify teachers that offer support and expertise. – Experienced teachers—continue to offer individualized support.
How are you clearly defining their roles and expectations of their performance?
– Monthly grade-level and data meetings. – Outline and monitor student academic and behavioral success.
How do you ensure teachers have access to curriculum and assess learning?
– Beginning of the year make sure they have all of the necessary resources. – Monthly data meetings to discuss the need for additional services/resources.
How do you ensure that they have the tools and resources for success?
– Start with foundational resources. – Give professional leeway to incorporate different materials to elicit enhanced student learning. – Purchase additional tools and materials as needed.
How do your teachers use data to guide classroom instruction?
– Each student has individual baseline and growth target scores in each content area. – Teachers use resources to monitor their progress. – Progress monitoring results discussed at monthly data meetings.
How do you facilitate the occurrence of mentoring and collaboration?
– Pair teachers together based on similar content and characteristics. – Encourage formal and informal groups to collaborate on student needs.
How do you grow teachers professionally, both individually and collectively?
– Bring professional development into school for the group. – Target individual teacher needs, as they arise or are requested.

A Genuine Leader . . .

A genuine leader understands that teacher satisfaction within the learning environment has a positive effect on student success. The leadership style and influence that the school leader engages in directly impacts that working environment. Ultimately, school leaders who focus on student success, and teacher satisfaction as a means to influence student success, increase the likelihood of cultivating that success in the daily lives of their students. By taking the time to create and cultivate teacher satisfaction, and its connection to student academic success, you are taking a significant step towards becoming that genuine leader.

To truly be satisfied, I must find value AND be valued in what I do.

CHAPTER TAKEAWAYS

Takeaway Tidbit

- Being open, honest, accessible, and compassionate to the needs of the teachers increases their satisfaction, which has a direct impact on student success.

Takeaway Templates

- Cultivating Teacher Satisfaction Template 11.1 (eResource M).

Takeaway Tasks

- Complete the Cultivating Teacher Satisfaction Activity.
- Complete the Moment of Reflection.

Moment of Reflection . . .

Reflect on how satisfied your teachers are with their work environment and your leadership. Do you really know their level of satisfaction? What processes could you have in place to gauge that level, so that you can support their needs? What avenues do they have to reach you? To what degree are you comfortable with supporting teacher satisfaction? How does it feed or starve teacher satisfaction?

_____

_____

_____

_____

_____

References

Amoroso, P. (2005). Putting words into action. *Principal Leadership: Middle Level Edition, 5*(9), 27–29.

Angelle, P. (2006). Instructional leadership and monitoring: Increasing teacher intent to stay through socialization. *NASSP Bulletin, 90*(4), 318–334.

Black, S. (2004). Great beginnings. *American School Board Journal, 191*(10), 44–46.

Bodycott, P., Walker, A., & Lee Chi Kin, J. (2001). More than heroes and villains: Pre-service teacher beliefs about principals. *Educational Research, 43*(1), 15–17.

Brendle-Corum, A., & Haynes, J. (2004). Four ways to support new teachers. *Principal, 84*(1), 61.

Brock, B., & Grady, M. (2007). *From first-year to first rate: Principals guiding beginning teachers.* Thousand Oaks, CA: Corwin Press.

Cheng, M., & Cheung, W. (2004). Comparing perceptions: The competence of novice teachers and the expectations of school principals. *Asia Pacific Education Review, 5*(1), 188–199.

Davis, B., & Bloom, G. (1998). Support new teachers. *Thrust for Educational Leadership, 28*(2), 16–18.

DePaul, A. (2005). How new teachers can enlist the help they need. *Curriculum Review, 45*(3), 7–8.

Ganser, T. (2002). Building the capacity of school districts to design, implement, and evaluate effective new teacher mentor programs: Action points for colleges and universities. *Mentoring & Tutoring: Partnership in Learning, 10*(1), 47–55.

Gimbert, B., & Fultz, D. (2009). Top 10 actions a principal can do to make my first year successful. *Principal's Office.* Retrieved from http://principalsoffice.osu.edu/files/staff.9.09.php

Johnson, S., & Kardos, S. (2005). Bridging the generation gap. *Educational Leadership, 62*(8), 8–14.

Kardos, S., Johnson, S., Peske, H., Kauffman, D., & Liu, E. (2001). Counting on colleagues: New teachers encounter the professional cultures of their schools. *Educational Administration Quarterly, 37*(2), 250.

Mauer, E., & Zimmerman, E. (2000). Mentoring new teachers. *Principal, 79*(3), 26–28.

McCann, T., Johannessen, L., & Ricca, B. (2005). Responding to new teachers' concerns. *Educational Leadership, 62*(8), 30–34.

McKerrow, K. (1996). Support then solutions: The supervision of teachers. *Clearing House, 69*(6), 330–332.

Melton, A. A. (2007). *An exploratory study of the dyadic relationship of the beginning teacher and the administrator.* Unpublished Doctoral Dissertation. Michigan State University, Lansing, MI.

Menchaca, V. (2003). A wake-up call for principals: Are your novice teachers leaving? *Catalyst for Change, 33*(1), 25.

Quinn, R., & Andrews, B. (2004). The struggles of first-year teachers investigating support mechanism. *Clearing House, 77*(4), 164–169.

Renwick, L. (2007). Keeping new teachers happy. *District Administration, 43*(1), 26.

Richards, J. (2004). What new teachers value most in principals. *Principal, 83*(3), 42–44.

Ruder, R. (2005). What to do when the brightest begin to dim. *Principal Leadership, 5*(8), 28–29.

Seashore Louis, K., Leithwood, K., Wahlstrom, K., & Anderson, S. (2010). *Investigating the links to improved student learning.* Retrieved

June 3, 2010 from http://www.wallacefoundation.org/KnowledgeCenter/KnowledgeTopics/CurrentAreasofFocus/EducationLeadership/Pages/learning-from-leadership-investigating-the-links-to-improved-student-learning.aspx

Smith, A., Morrow, J., & Gray, D. (1999). Principals educate beginning teachers about the law. *Education, 120*(1), 60.

Stansbury, K. (2001). What new teachers need. *Leadership, 30*(3), 18.

Walsdorf, K., & Lynn, S. (2002). The early years: Mediating the organizational environment. *Clearing House, 75*(4), 90–94.

Watkins, P. (2005). The principal's role in attracting, retaining, and developing new teachers. *Clearing House, 79*(2), 83–87.

Wayne, A., Youngs, P., & Fleischman, S. (2005). Improving teacher induction. *Educational Leadership, 62*(8), 76–78.

Wong, H. (2004). Induction programs that keep new teachers teaching and improving. *NASSP Bulletin, 88*(638), 41–58.

Wood, A. (2005). The importance of principals: Site administrators' role in novice teacher induction. *American Secondary Education, 33*(2), 39–62.

PART

1 Rule

1 Rule

1. Treat Others Like You Want to be Treated

Merriam-Webster (2015a) defines the word **rule** as, "A prescribed guide for conduct or action." This section discusses the 1 rule that you as the genuine leader must follow in order to facilitate a healthy and successful school environment.

Step 10

Treat Others Like You Want to Be Treated

The Golden Rule.

The tenth step, and first rule that guides your conduct and action, is treating others like you want to be treated. The single most important thing that you can do as a genuine leader is to treat everyone with the same respect that you expect from others toward you. The following five sub-rules to Step 10 will help guide you in reflecting on the level and degree of implementation of this step in your daily practices as the school leader.

Be Trusting If You Want to Be Trusted

Trust is a power thing. Merriam-Webster (2015b) defines **trust** as having, "Confidence or faith in something or someone." There is nothing more powerful than having a staff willing to have confidence and faith that you are making the right decisions and leading them in the right direction. Also, many decisions come down from the district office that will require the school leader to make certain decisions or mandate a certain process or policy that may not be easily understood by the staff. They need to trust that you as the school leader will look out for their best interests and, more importantly, the best interests of the children, without leading them in the wrong direction.

Know that trust is a two-way street. Teachers will not have trust in you until you show that you have trust in them. Put teachers in positions to earn your trust and acknowledge how much you trust them while they are in that position. This builds their self-efficacy, as well as a relationship of trust with you. Once trust is established, collectively you will be able to move mountains.

Be Respectful If You Want to Be Respected

Let's be clear, there are two different types of respect: respect for the position (title respect) and respect for the person (individual respect). Title respect for the school leader is often superficial and formal. The teachers and staff may follow your directions simply due to the fact that you are the school leader. Their level and degree of commitment may not be as strong as you want, but at least at face value you being the boss will get them to comply.

What I am really focusing on here is gaining individual respect. It is important to have the teachers and staff respect you as an individual first, and as the school leader second. With respect comes loyalty and commitment. Teachers are asked to perform a variety of functions and duties both inside the school setting and outside in the larger community. Their loyalty to you and the vision and mission of the school in which you lead are reflected in the community. There are teachers in some school settings who will perform their best as an ambassador for their school leader, and teachers who will perform their best in spite of their school leader.

You as the school leader may initially be given title respect regardless of how you act towards your teachers and staff. However, if you want to gain individual respect you must first show respect to them. Respect must be given before it is ever earned. Teachers are professionals who attended college, many even have advanced degrees, and entered a workforce that is not financially lucrative and often comes with very little positive incentives and benefits. You as the school leader have an opportunity to openly acknowledge them with the respect that they crave and motivate them to reach higher levels of success for themselves, as well as their students. By setting the example of how to show respect, you build the exchange framework were respect can be connected and reciprocated. You also lay the foundation for demonstrating to them how to convey that same respect to their students. Either way, you must first show respect if you want to be shown respect.

Be Kind and Compassionate If You Want to Be Treated with Kindness and Compassion

Being a school leader can be a very lonely position, especially if you are the only administrator in the building. You have to manage the physical facilities, deal with parental concerns, attend community functions, and support teacher needs and student concerns. You cannot have a bad day, as all of your actions are scrutinized by someone and decisions are criticized by those who do not immediately benefit from your choices. No matter how professional we try to be during work hours, we are humans with our own issues, struggles, uncertainties, and bad days. When "life" happens, we attempt to adjust our mindsets or actions in order to deal with the chaos invading our lives at that particular moment. In these times it is wonderful to have teachers and staff show kindness and compassion towards you, understanding what you are going through and offering support. When you have a support structure in place, you can rely on individuals to help carry the burden so that you can focus on the most important things first until you have addressed all issues and concerns.

However, kindness and compassion are reciprocal, and are often not the focus of effective leadership. In order for you as the school leader to be treated with kindness and compassion, you must first create and maintain a healthy work environment by showing kindness and compassion to your teachers and staff. The school leader must understand this and display kindness, concern, and compassion during times of struggle. This is not to say that the school leader should excuse the chaotic craziness that interferes with educating students. Quite the opposite: if they understand the situation and provide support, or at least a comforting ear, the teachers may feel more empowered to perform their duties at a higher level knowing that the school leader isn't criticizing everything and is cheering them on. The point here is to be kind and compassionate if you want to be treated with kindness and compassion.

Be Fair If You Want to Be Treated with Fairness

There will be times when teachers and staff will make snap judgments about your decisions without ever truly understanding the complexities of your decision-making process. They are not privy to that process and often if the decision doesn't go their way, they are not concerned with how you arrived at what they consider the "wrong" conclusion. They most likely will voice their opinions to all who will listen in an attempt to sway their fellow colleagues into siding with them on your incompetency. All of a sudden there is a question of fairness to these actions. As a school leader, you must make the tough decisions, and in some instances the best decision is not the most popular one, but you have to make it anyway. You attempt to explain your decision-making process and the reasoning as to why you made that specific choice. You then hope that your teachers and staff see the fairness and rationality in your decision and accept it without the negative propaganda being spread all through the work environment. Although you can't always avoid this, the best way for you to minimize these occurrences is by building a reputation of being fair in your decisions. This is done by treating others with fairness.

Teachers and staff want to know that in the greater scheme of the educational environment, they are being treated fairly. Fairness is such a subjective word that can mean many things. I like to define fairness in terms of equity rather than equality. Teachers must feel that you are providing support that fits their individual needs. For example, your 3rd grade classroom needs math computer software to assist in targeting their individual math levels and remediate the areas in which they are struggling, while your art class needs more colored pencils and sketch pads. You do not go out and buy both classes art supplies and computer software. That would be treating them equal but not fair. Instead, you secure the art supplies for the art room and the software for the math class. That is both equitable and fair, as you address their specific needs. This also holds true with whomever you select to be your advisory staff, team leaders, conference attenders, etc. If you are not making these selections in a fair and systematic way, you run the risk of being labeled as someone who is unfair. If teachers feel that you are treating them and their colleagues with fairness, they will give you the benefit of the doubt about decisions that don't always go their way. The bottom line here is if you want to be treated fair, you must first treat others with fairness.

Be the Type of Leader That You Want to Follow

Be the type of leader that you want to follow. Before you make a decision or engage in an action, ask yourself if YOU would follow you into this educational battle. Would you be proud of your school leader for making this decision? Would you think that this was fair, compassionate, respectful and trustworthy? How would you need to have it explained to you in order for it to make sense? Did you explain it to your staff so that it made sense to them? I know these questions seem endless, but if you want to have the type of environment that is conducive for success, you as the school leader must commit the time and energy into building a genuine leadership environment where "because I said so" has no place to exist. Check yourself in that mirror by asking, "Am I the type of leader that I would follow?" If that answer is no, then why should you expect others to follow you? Become the leader that your teachers need and your students deserve.

Use Template 12.1 to walk you through how you as the school leader engage and interact with other teachers and staff. The example below illustrates how to use this template.

Template 12.1 Be That Type of Leader

How are you conveying trust and demonstrating you can be trusted?
– Treat teachers as professionals. – Don't micromanage their time and schedule. – Accept their recommendations when appropriate.
How are you conveying respect, and demonstrating you can be respected?
– Put them into positions to lead groups and make recommendations.
How are you conveying compassion, and demonstrating you can be compassionate?
– Care about their families and life outside of the workplace. – Be flexible and understanding when emergencies arise.
How are you conveying fairness, and demonstrating you can be fair?
– Listen to their side of the issues and consider their feelings. – Look for win-win situations. – Explain in detail why you made your decisions.
How can you better demonstrate the type of leader that you want to follow?
– Never ask staff to perform any duty or activity that you are not willing to perform first. – Be both professional and caring when interacting with staff.

A Genuine Leader . . .

A genuine leader understands that it's about how you as the school leader approach the relationship aspects of leading your staff. There are times when we feel uncomfortable reflecting on our relationship practices and therefore only skim over it or ignore it altogether. A genuine leader must resist the urge to do this, and force themselves into that uncomfortable moment for the purpose of self-evaluation and enlightenment. By taking the time to mindfully reflect on how you engage and interact with others, you are taking a significant step towards becoming that genuine leader.

> Be trusting if you want to be trusted.
> Be respectful if you want to be respected.
> Be compassionate if you want to be shown compassion.
> Be fair if you want to be treated with fairness.
> Be the type of leader that you want to follow.

CHAPTER TAKEAWAYS

Takeaway Tidbit

- Treat others how you would like to be treated.

Takeaway Templates

- Be That Type of Leader Template 12.1 (eResource N).

Takeaway Tasks

- Complete the Be That Type of Leader Activity.
- Complete the Moment of Reflection.

Moment of Reflection . . .

Reflect on how you demonstrate trust, respect, compassion, and fairness to staff and students. How can you improve upon what you already have in place? What areas need more work? How will you engage in professional development to enhance these areas?

_____

_____

_____

_____

_____

References

Merriam-Webster. (2015a). *Rule*. Retrieved November 15, 2014 from http://www.merriam-webster.com/dictionary/principle

Merriam-Webster. (2015b). *Trust*. Retrieved November 15, 2014 from http://www.merriam-webster.com/dictionary/trust

13

Conclusion: Why Genuine Leadership?

A genuine leader exhibits a clear and straightforward steward-ship of education.

The basic premise of genuine leadership is the sharing of how we engage and develop students in order to comprehensively meet their individual needs. It's that interactive relationship built upon trust, honesty, respect, allocation of resources, and the collective understanding of the vision and mission of the school. The principal remains the pinnacle of authority and decision-making, but defers to those educators who have the expertise, resources, buy-in, and community connections to build a collective capacity of serving student needs at all grade levels. This decision-making structure allows for the multiple exchange of information and ideas, increasing awareness of differentiated learning and implementing a more comprehensive plan of instructional delivery, ultimately increasing the effectiveness of the school's ability to cultivate student success.

The 10 steps detailed in this book all play a codependent role within the genuine leadership approach of growing students and running a school. When reflecting upon the contexts of each of these steps through the lens of genuine leadership, there is a clear picture of why communication, empowerment, and the sharing of decision-making are paramount to reach student academic needs.

4 Principles

Step 1: Keep Your Focus on the Child
Step 2: Share Your Vision, NOT Your Brain

Step 3: Understand That Absolute Power Corrupts Absolutely
Step 4: Education Is a "Contact" Sport

The school leader must keep their focus on the child. When outside demands and distractions pull the leader's focus away from the child, he or she must count upon their colleagues to pull that focus back on the student. Genuine leadership facilitates a process in which teachers can hold the school leader accountable for that focus, without fear of punitive retribution. The vison is shared so that it can be comprehensively reviewed, making sure that different perspectives have input and that all pieces have been considered. Decision-making itself is shared and harbored with the ones that have the expertise and closest connection with the issue, all under the purview of the school leader. Genuine leadership encourages the connectivity between student, teacher, parent, and community. Parental and community involvement is paramount to student and school success. It encourages and supports teachers reaching out to their circles of influence outside of the school for support and resources that meet student needs.

3 Processes

Step 5: Know What You Have / What You Need
Step 6: Building Network Capacity
Step 7: Know Your Role

Genuine leadership is about engaging teachers and support staff in taking a hard look at what the school is doing well and what needs to be addressed. It facilitates the growth of both the internal and external network as a way to support students. It also keeps in focus that the school leader does not have to be the leader of every initiative at every meeting. It empowers and accommodates teacher leadership and ownership of their work environment, increasing buy-in, motivation, and ultimately higher levels of teacher satisfaction.

2 Goals

Step 8: Cultivate Student Success
Step 9: Cultivate Teacher Satisfaction

Genuine leadership directly influences student success and teacher satisfaction. The teachers are in the classroom teaching, assessing, and reflecting on best practice for students. They are on the front lines making decisions that affect student learning. Listening to their needs, assisting with solutions and resources, and supporting their daily ways of practice are paramount to student success. Likewise, if teachers do not feel like they are supported and valued, student learning suffers. They must find satisfaction in what they do in order to keep doing it well. School climate impacts both teacher satisfaction and student achievement. Without that network of communi cation, collaboration, and empowerment, student success suffers.

1 Rule

Step 10: Treat Others Like You Want to Be Treated

Genuine leadership builds capacity of trust, mutual respect, ownership, collaboration, and value. By developing these interconnected relation- ships, the school leader and teachers understand each other and rally around a common vision for the school and its respected students. Treating others like you want to be treated is a foundational human concept that spans centuries. When achieved within a genuine, healthy environment, the school and all its inhabitants show success.

Be the Genuine Leader

A genuine leader exhibits that clear and straightforward stewardship of education through the tight and loosely connected relationships between concepts, content, and people that support student success. When school leaders engage in this type of approach to leadership, they cultivate a school climate in which the teachers are impacted by the influence of the collective capacity of the school community, which in turn evokes posi- tive outcomes on student academic success (Seashore Louis, Leithwood, Wahlstrom, & Anderson, 2010). The school leader has the greatest impact on student academic success through building school capacity, fostering teacher knowledge development, and supporting teacher-led collaborative learning and decision-making teams. In this manner, the principal facili- tates the networking of ideas, practices, processes, and supports so that students reap the benefits of efficient and effective exchanges of teaching information, techniques, and best practices.

Ultimately, this approach to leadership is meant to be a guide to both new and experienced school leaders who are working in collaboration with their staff on providing a more effective educational environment for their students. Likewise, this approach supports the school leader in providing a structure that acknowledges and celebrates teacher ownership of student engagement, along with the mentality that we are all in this together. Margaret Mead (BrainyQuote, 2015) once declared, "Never doubt that a small group of thoughtful, committed citizens can change the world; indeed, it's the only thing that ever has." Commit today to change the world through your actions, for you may be the linchpin between a child and their successful future. Be that "genuine leader" that your school needs, and your students deserve!

Final Moment of Reflection . . .

Final Moment of Reflection . . .

After completing the book, reflect on the top three things that you learned. What is your plan to take the knowledge gained from this book and reflect it in your daily practices? What initial steps do you need to take in order to become that genuine leader?

_____

_____

_____

_____

_____

References

BrainyQuote. (2015). Retrieved October 23, 2015 from http://www.brainyquote.com/quotes/quotes/m/margaretme100502.html

Seashore Louis, K., Leithwood, K., Wahlstrom, K., & Anderson, S. (2010). _Investigating the links to improved student learning_. Retrieved June 3, 2010 from http://www.wallacefoundation.org/KnowledgeCenter/KnowledgeTopics/CurrentAreasofFocus/EducationLeadership/Pages/learning-from-leadership-investigating-the-links-to-improved-student-learning.aspx